How to Grow Your Business Using
LinkedIn™

Compiled, Edited and Written by

Bruce 'Zen' Benefiel, MA, MBA

Socially Mediated Extrovert and Possibilities Coagulator

Published by Be The Dream LLC

Copyright where applicable ©2014

ISBN-13:
978-1499145045

ISBN-10:
1499145047

PRO President's vision and goal is to help small businesses succeed. PRO's primary activity is the creation and facilitation of peer advisory boards for small business owners and key executives.

In a world of fast changing business environment, PRO also recognizes the need to bring insight and new concepts to the small business community. The workshop "Is LinkedIn Getting You More Business?" is an example of the information PRO, President's fosters. Zen Benefiel's expertise and this workbook made it possible.

Marketing and sales have changed from the historic format. Today, it is much harder to generate and create relationship sales. It is much harder to make personal contact or phone contact. Business people must learn and use additional techniques. This workbook outlines some of the ideas.

I personally have changed my marketing and sales strategy and method of going to market. Being an "old dog" I must learn new tricks. LinkedIn and various implementation concepts are the new tricks. I use Zen as my digital guru.

Please review and use this material. We would be happy to discuss the concepts and how PRO can create greater value and benefits for you. We also have a small business radio show called 2 Small Biz Guys where we discuss many tasty business tidbits. Find us on 2SmallBizGuys.com for on-demand listening.

Cultivating Business Success,

Ray Silverstein

Founder and President
PRO, President's Resource Organization
www.propres.com
ray@propres.com
800 818-0150

Contents

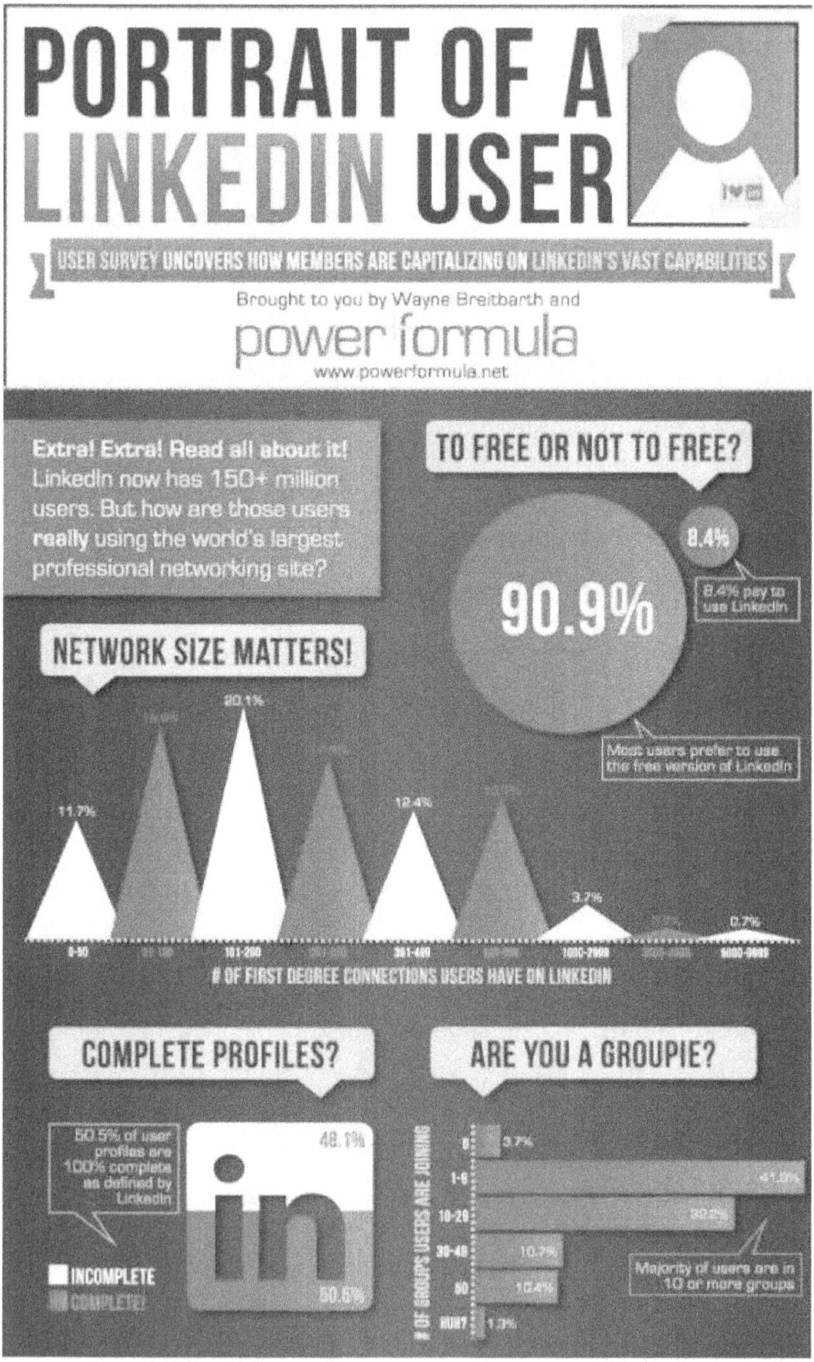

PORTRAIT OF A LINKEDIN USER

Brought to you by Wayne Breitbarth and

power formula
www.powerformula.net

Extra! Extra! Read all about it! LinkedIn now has 150+ million users. But how are those users **really** using the world's largest professional networking site?

TO FREE OR NOT TO FREE?

8.4%

90.9%

8.4% pay to use LinkedIn

Most users prefer to use the free version of LinkedIn

NETWORK SIZE MATTERS!

20.1%

11.7%

12.4%

3.7%

0.7%

0-50   101-200   351-400   1000-2000   5000-9999

OF FIRST DEGREE CONNECTIONS USERS HAVE ON LINKEDIN

COMPLETE PROFILES?

50.5% of user profiles are 100% complete as defined by LinkedIn

48.1%

in

■ INCOMPLETE
■ COMPLETE

50.5%

ARE YOU A GROUPIE?

OF GROUPS USERS ARE JOINING

0   3.7%

1-6   41.9%

10-20   30.2%

30-49   10.7%

50   10.4%

HUH?   1.3%

Majority of users are in 10 or more groups

2

Getting the Gold

You are about to embark on a journey into cyberspace, specifically into the realms of LinkedIn™ and its many features. As you might imagine, no one person or book has all the answers. In this book we'll look at information collected from a number of sources, plus offer some wisdom regarding relationship building.

Mining for gold in this environment is about creating relationships: establishing credibility, finding decision-makers and closing sales. It all sounds so sterile, but the sales cycle is anything but clean and clear. Many salespeople forget that the person on the other end has priorities, too, and the 'job' is transferring the enthusiasm in order to shift those priorities. Sales come by asking the questions. Every question has an answer. Are you asking the right ones?

In this workbook we will explore some of those 'right' questions that lead you to the best answers; people, places and things that fill your sales pipeline and reward you with deals that close more often than not. The manner in which you conduct your sales efforts is important. We will not attempt to tell you how to sell, although we might offer some refreshments that whet your appetite for getting better.

Our goals for you:

- Build an Excellent Personal Profile
- Build a Company Profile
- Create Product/Service Listing
- Install Video message
- Use Advanced Features for Research & Networking
- Use LinkedIn™ Groups for Client Development and Outreach
- Garner Recommendations and Referrals
- Connect with Decision Makers
- Develop Relationships that Grow Your Business

Some interesting tidbits on LinkedIn:

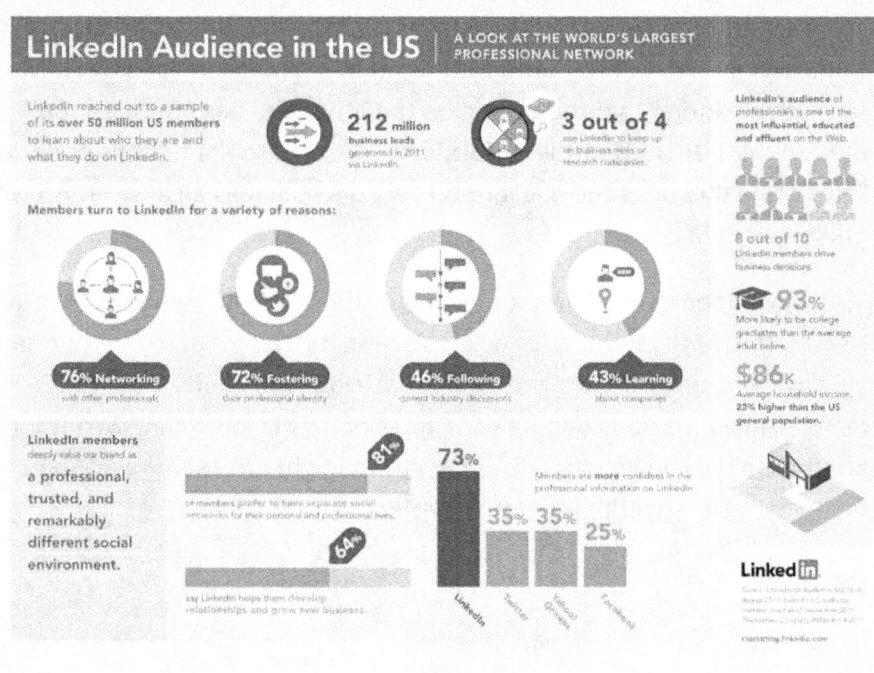

Where Are You Going?

Goals are reached by setting them, first. All the master-planners and successful entrepreneurs state that visualizing the end product, the goal achieved, is the best place to start. Goals are dreams with deadlines.

So, what does your vision look like? (use timeframes, too)

_____

_____

_____

_____

_____

_____

_____

_____

_____

_____

_____

_____

_____

_____

_____

_____

_____

_____

_____

_____

It may seem odd to start out an exploration into LinkedIn™ with a request to journal your vision. However, it is much easier to set up a strategy when you know what you want to achieve. Take a moment and consider the value of what you have in front of you - the LinkedIn™ resource.

What are your goals for using the resource?

1) _____

2) _____

3) _____

4) _____

How do you think you can achieve your goals? Keep in mind there may be multiple steps to single items. Like many results, there are multiple ways of achieving them. The better questions you formulate in the 'How do I...?" stage, the better your results will be. Speed is not always the best thing. If you are dealing with people, building solid relationships may take more time than you anticipate.

Perhaps looking at this project, your closed deals, we can begin with a view from above – the work breakdown structure. It is the critical path that you will take in order to achieve your goals. It applies to any endeavor and, according to the experts: whatever time you think it will take is best tripled for optimum stress-free performance.

Action plans are simple work breakdown structures that are step-by-step initiatives for accomplishing goals. We do not suggest that this is not obvious, but we do want to remind you that it is important to remember. Sometimes our progress is hindered by small things we forget to do. Sales are systematic, they follow a predictable course. So does building relationships. As a well-known local sales coach, Allan Himmelstein, says, "Sales is not a dirty work; just a higher level of communication."

What can you do?

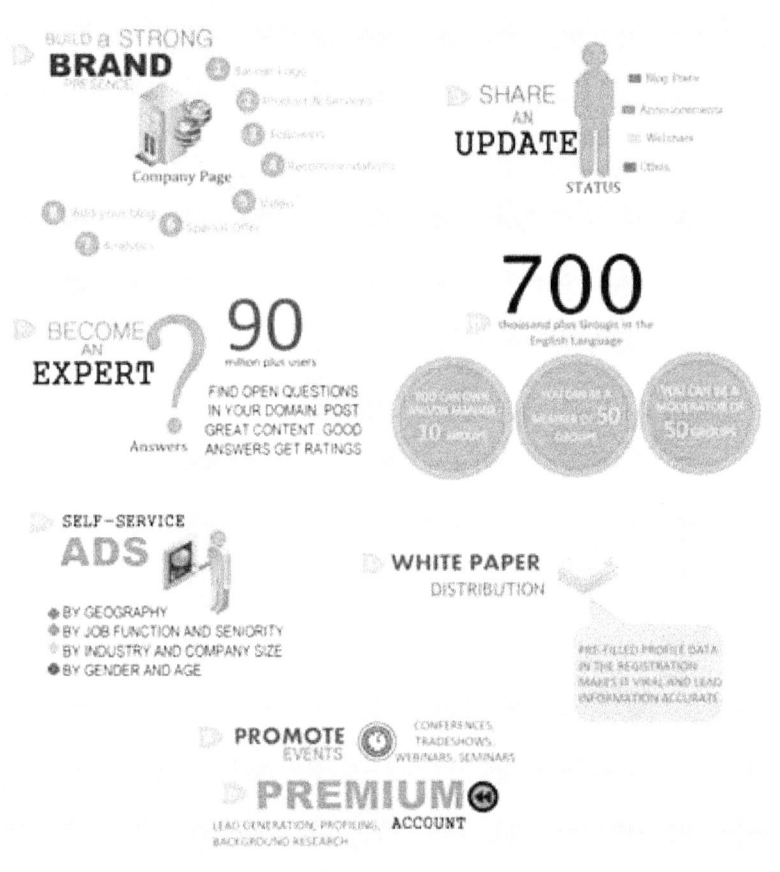

Relative statistics as of 2012:

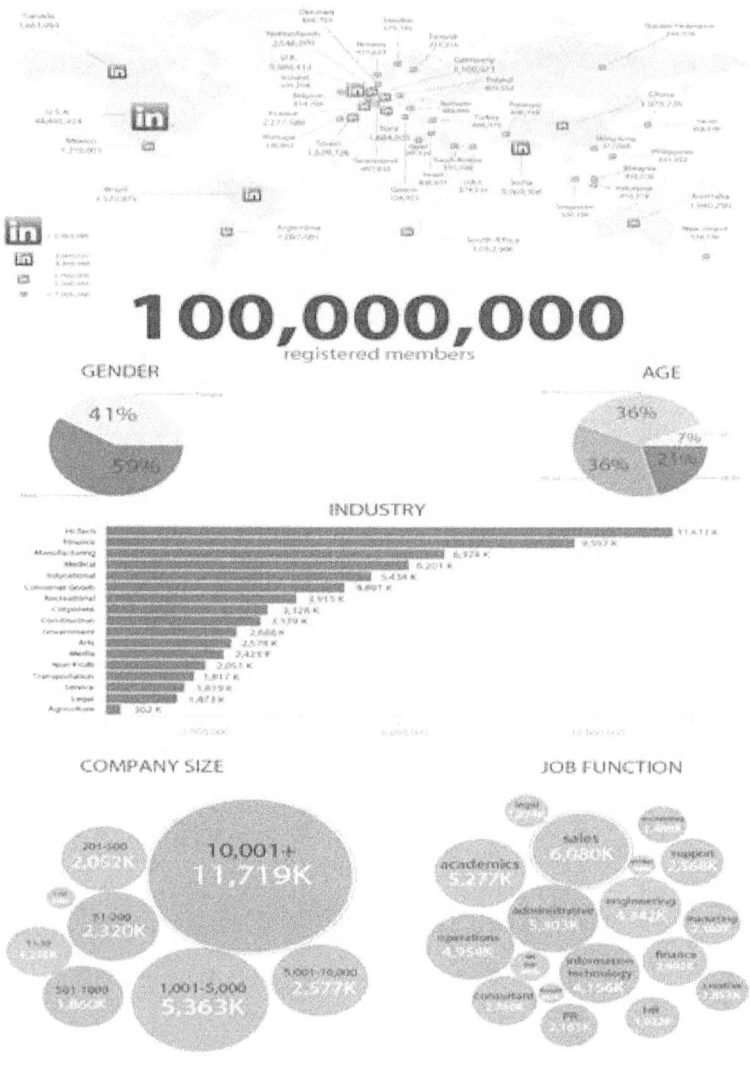

Personal Profiles

Depending on your purpose and strategy on LinkedIn™, your profile should reflect the ultimate in professionalism and your personal style. It's best to be authentic and honest, but you don't have to fully disclose. Think about what you are doing, *clients and customers that are going to be attracted* and the overall message you want them to get from viewing your profile.

For the purpose of this workbook, you are an entrepreneur. Salespeople are entrepreneurs who put people, places and things together to do business. If you are selling a product or service then you need to be clear in describing what that is and offering features and benefits of YOUR SERVICE. It is your service to your clients and customers that will engage them.

CREATE YOUR PROFESSIONAL HEADLINE

Tune in to that creative universe within you and...

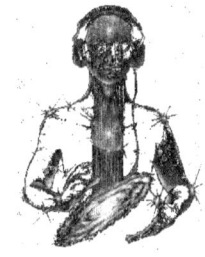

Character Limit: 120 (including spaces)

What words best capture your job title and target industry/market (e.g., Hotshot Health Hero, Software Rockstar, Risk Aversion Czar, Creative Consultant, Vehicle Virtuoso)?

Example:

Gregarious Programmer with a penchant for connecting clients with technical service professionals that ROCK.

Take a moment and create your own...

_____

_____

_____

_____

_____

Think about a few keywords or phrases that OTHERS might use to describe your service and write them down here: (use a separate sheet if needed)

1) _____

2) _____

3) _____

4) _____

5) _____

Think about a few keywords or phrases that YOU might use to describe your service and write them down here: (use a separate sheet if needed)

1) _____

2) _____

3) _____

4) _____

5) _____

Use those keywords in developing your profile description. You will want to make sure that they are terms that are congruent with your business persona and style. Tell a story with your client or customer as a featured guest and you as the ultimate servant for their particular needs. Be creative. You'll stand out in the crowd.

Other things you'll want to consider are your accomplishments, examples of best-practices in your field, advanced training or degrees and short impactful testimonials. If you feel you cannot write about yourself in a way that feels authentic and creative, hire a coach to help you. Sometimes they are worth their weight in gold… especially when you get the gold as a result. Keep in mind this is an on-going work-in-progress as you develop.

A good rule of thumb is to write short paragraphs, three to five sentences, which demonstrate your understanding of grammar and mechanics. You can use bullet points for specific details or itemized lists. Good flow will capture your readers and draw them into the reading. Proper paragraph structure includes topic sentences that are backed up with content that supports them and closes with a restatement of the topic sentence.

For example:

My clients/customers love how I tailor-make presentations to their specific needs. Doing research to understand a client/customer problem allows me to know more about their business. It automatically builds rapport and our business relationship takes on a higher degree of trust. I can suggest options and they will listen, providing better results. "Joe really got to know our business." (Sam S., owner of XYZ services)

Here's an article from SalesForce.com (with corrections) that offers more:

Improve Your LinkedIn™ Profile, Improve Your Sales Results
by Kevin Micalizzi, Data.com Social Media Marketing Manager

When you come across someone new in your daily routine as a sales person, I'm guessing you look them up on LinkedIn™ to get a better idea of their background. Correspondingly, a lot of your customers and prospects are checking you out on LinkedIn™ and it's crucial to convey that you are good at your job and a sales person they can trust.

However if you follow the majority of the LinkedIn™ profile advice that's been published, the chances are you look more like you're job hunting than like you are successful at selling.

With the recent LinkedIn™ profile redesign, you have a great opportunity to put the right image forward, so here are some tips for making sure your profile says the right thing about you.

1. Show some personality (and your face)

There's plenty of advice out there about the perfect LinkedIn™ profile photo. The most important to me is that people connect with people. Make sure your photo clearly shows your face. Unless you're in an industry where everyone dresses formal, use a more business casual photo. It lets you appear approachable while still looking professional. And make sure you smile.

Sophia Browning

Account Executive with preference for hunting over farming

San Francisco Bay Area | Online Media

Current	Account Executive at Salesforce.com
Previous	Salesforce.com, Cooliris, CNN
Education	MA, International Policy Studies at Stanford University

Improve your profile

387
connections

2. Rock it with a great headline & summary

Your headline is one of the first things people see about you. Go beyond your job title. Most job titles never truly describe what you do anyways. Use the keywords your customers would search for, not the terms your company may use. And remember, professional headlines sell.

My favorite advice on making your profile a marketing workhorse for you is to use the summary to add a personal intro about your goals, what you're passionate about, and what you love to do in life. This lets people see you as a well-rounded person.

3. This isn't your resume, don't drown us in details

I recommend removing job descriptions from your past experience. Unless you're job hunting, I see this section used more often as a way to verify that you're not new to your current sales role and that you're reliable. You want your experience to help emphasize you're not going to sell something and then vanish.

4. Share your skills

You've probably seen people endorsing your skills on LinkedIn™, I know I have. It's an interesting new feature but honestly, not all the "skills" LinkedIn™ is suggesting to people are things I'd consider important. Add some key skills to your profile to ensure LinkedIn™ is asking your connections to endorse you on things that are relevant to what you do.

5. What do your groups say about you?

We've all joined LinkedIn™ groups we find interesting and/or relevant. Take a look at your public profile to see what groups are listed. Do they reflect the image you want to portray? For any that aren't adding value to your image, go into Your Settings for any of the groups you belong to and uncheck the "Display the group logo on your profile" option. Some people may disagree with me, but I put college and company alumni groups in this category, your profile already shows your employment and education history.

6. Are you like-able?

With LinkedIn™, once you pass 500 connections, your profile will show 500+ connections. Try to get past 500, even if you're only slightly over, it helps you to appear well connected. Recommendations also give you a bit of "social proof", letting people who don't know you see that others feel you are worth working with. Make sure everyone is a real recommendation. No one is fooled by a number of people recommending you with things like, "she's awesome", or "he was great to work with." If you ask for a recommendation (or get one without asking), don't be afraid to ask the person recommending you to talk about something specific. In my experience, if they're willing to write a recommendation, they're happy to give it some focus. And the more focused the reviews are, the more meaningful they'll be to people who check out your profile.

What else have you found helps your LinkedIn™ profile work for your sales?

If you are looking for sales opportunities or positions, then you will want to craft your profile with a focus on your skill set and track record.

From, **Wayne Breitbarth**, an apparent LinkedIn™ Author/Speaker/Trainer...

How will I know I am making progress on LinkedIn™?

If you are really honest with yourself, you have probably asked yourself this very legitimate question. The ultimate answer should be: If you're accomplishing the LinkedIn™ goals you've set, then you're making progress.

And the most common goals I hear are:

- generate customer leads
- find a job
- increase my brand
- improve my presence
- find donors or volunteers

Trust me, I hear success stories for each of these every week, but it sometimes takes time to see the progress. So, while you are on that journey, what numbers should you track to see if you are making progress?

Here is a list of the ten most important LinkedIn™ metrics you may want to start tracking as you work to accomplish your overall goal(s).

1. **# of connections.** This is the big one. In general, the bigger your network, the better off you are. Many of the metrics listed below will improve just by growing this number.

2. **# of connections in your targeted industries, companies, regions, etc**. To monitor this, you'll need to use LinkedIn™ tags to categorize your connections. Seeing these numbers go up will mean good things, because you can send targeted messages to these important groups of people.

3. **# of profile views.** The raw number is important here, but more important is who are these folks and what action steps (connect, message, etc.) did you take with the good ones. For more information on this highly rated feature, click here.

4. **# of times you showed up in a search.** This should increase not just from increasing the number of connections but having enough of your keywords in the right spots on your profile.

5. **# of invitations to connect**. If this number is increasing month over month, it usually means your activity level is increasing not only on LinkedIn™ itself but in your physical world as well.

6. **# of people viewing your updates**. If you haven't started using this section, you are missing the boat. Of course, you have to post status updates to get these metrics. It's a great way to see what type of updates are resonating with your audience and what time of the week might be your sweet spot for posting.

7. **# of people "liking," sharing or commenting on your updates**. Yes, the numbers are important here, but also consider reaching out to the people who share, "like" or comment on your updates. A simple thank you or sharing one of their insightful updates with your network would be noticed and appreciated, I'm sure.

8. **# of endorsements for your top ten skills** (keywords). I know you may be annoyed by the whole idea of endorsements (I'm with you), but LinkedIn™ loves these, and so I'm pretty sure that increasing your number of endorsements for the right skills is going to help you.

9. **# of recommendations**. Even though endorsements are all the buzz, recommendations are still extremely important for your overall social proof. Believe me, people do read these, especially if you're directing them to do so at some point in your conversation or relationship. Work hard at getting LinkedIn™ recommendations. It will be time well spent.

10. **# of hits to a website from LinkedIn™**. This could be from any shareable link you may have placed in the following LinkedIn™ profile sections or features:

- Contact Info section website entries
- Publications
- Projects
- Professional Gallery
- Group discussions started by you or answered by you
- Status updates shared by you or commented on by you

I suggest you set up a simple spreadsheet with any of these ten LinkedIn™ metrics you think are important to you. Decide how often you will update your spreadsheet, and then start tracking. I suggest you do it at least quarterly.

As you improve these ten numbers, I suspect you'll see tangible evidence of progress in reaching your LinkedIn™ goals. Good luck!

Your Video Message

Do you have a short video to feature? There is now a feature in LinkedIn™ to include video. There are many ways to present there. The Speakers Resource Organization created a challenge to its membership: a 10-second introduction. If you would like to see their examples, you can find them and more here: www.SpeakersResourceOrganization.com/our-presenters

You might get some ideas or you may already have a 30-second to one-minute video you can use. You will find the instructions on how to add it on you LinkedIn™ professional profile page. You can add videos in other areas as well and it is advisable to do so. You will get more attention, especially if the production quality is good and you are being natural in the video.

Slideshare

This is another great feature that allows you to share important presentations that you can direct clients or potential clients to view. Another advantage of this feature is you can access the presentations anywhere and not have to rely on carrying your own technology. It does require an Internet connection and some kind of interface. ☺

Reading List

Here is where you can share your favorites, industry-related material and professional development resources that others may enjoy. It is always good to show that you are a life-long learner. It builds respect.

Preparing a Company Profile

If you have a company, then this profile is equally as important as your personal profile. The two can even be linked together from your personal/professional profile page. You want to make sure you have a few things ready before your begin.

Here is a short list:

1) Standard Company logo – hi-res image 100x60 pixels
2) Square Logo 50x50 pixels
3) 974px by 330px images for your company, products and services
4) Professional video introduction
5) Company description that sizzles
6) Product/Service description that sells, but not overtly
7) Unique Selling Proposition – your simply sizzling hook

Your PERSONAL BRAND is an asset that incorporates appearance, knowledge, and actions that give rise to a uniquely distinguishable and indelible impression.

Wikipedia defines brand as the identity of a specific product, service, or business. It is the personality that identifies a product, service, or company (and, for purposes of our discussion, a person) and how it relates to key constituencies: customers, shareholders, investors, partners, staff, and yes, employers. Ideally, your LinkedIn™ profile is designed to create favorable impressions of those accessing it and make you not just memorable, but indelible. Everything you do and say on LinkedIn™ is a reflection of your personal brand. Therefore, critical thinking is required every time you log into your LinkedIn™ account and begin making choices as to how to connect with and engage others.

Unique Selling Proposition *(from Entrepreneur.com)*

Before you can begin to sell your product or service to anyone else, you have to sell yourself on it. This is especially important when your product or service is similar to those around you. Very few businesses are one-of-a-kind. Just look around you: How many clothing retailers, hardware stores, air conditioning installers and electricians are truly unique?

The key to effective selling in this situation is what advertising and marketing professionals call a "unique selling proposition" (USP). Unless you can pinpoint what makes your business unique in a world of homogeneous competitors, you cannot target your sales efforts successfully.

Pinpointing your USP requires some hard soul-searching and creativity. One way to start is to analyze how other companies use their USPs to their advantage. This requires careful analysis of other companies' ads and marketing messages. If you analyze what they say they sell, not just their product or service characteristics, you can learn a great deal about how companies distinguish themselves from competitors.

For example, Charles Revson, founder of Revlon, always used to say he sold hope, not makeup. Some airlines sell friendly service, while others sell on-time service. Neiman Marcus sells luxury, while Wal-Mart sells bargains. What do you sell?

Each of these is an example of a company that has found a USP "peg" on which to hang its marketing strategy. A business can peg its USP on product characteristics, price structure, placement strategy (location and distribution) or promotional strategy. These are what marketers call the "four P's" of marketing. They are manipulated to give a business a market position that sets it apart from the competition.

Sometimes a company focuses on one particular "peg," which also drives the strategy in other areas. A classic example is Hanes L'Eggs hosiery. Back in an era when hosiery was sold primarily in department stores, Hanes opened a new distribution channel for hosiery sales. The idea: Since hosiery was a consumer staple, why not sell it where other staples were sold--in grocery stores?

That placement strategy then drove the company's selection of product packaging (a plastic egg) so the pantyhose did not seem incongruent in the supermarket. And because the product didn't have to be pressed and wrapped in tissue and boxes, it could be priced lower than other brands.

Here's how to uncover your USP and use it to power up your sales:

Put yourself in your customer's shoes. Too often, entrepreneurs fall in love with their product or service and forget that it is the customer's needs, not their own, that they must satisfy. Step back from your daily operations and carefully scrutinize what your customers really want. Suppose you own a pizza parlor. Sure, customers come into your pizza place for food. But is food all they want? What could make them come back again and again and ignore your competition? The answer might be quality, convenience, reliability, friendliness, cleanliness, courtesy or customer service.

Remember, price is never the only reason people buy. If your competition is beating you on pricing because they are larger, you have to find another sales feature that addresses the customer's needs and then build your sales and promotional efforts around that feature.

Know what motivates your customers' behavior and buying decisions. Effective marketing requires you to be an amateur psychologist. You need to know what drives and motivates customers. Go beyond the traditional customer demographics, such as age, gender, race, income and geographic location that most businesses collect to analyze their sales trends. For our pizza shop example, it is not enough to know that 75 percent of your customers are in the 18-to-25 age range. You need to look at their motives for buying pizza-taste, peer pressure, convenience and so on.

Cosmetics and liquor companies are great examples of industries that know the value of psychologically oriented promotion. People buy these products based on their desires (for pretty women, luxury, glamour and so on), not on their needs.

Uncover the real reasons customers buy your product. As your business grows, you'll be able to ask your best source of information: your customers. For example, the pizza entrepreneur could ask them why *they like his pizza over others, plus ask them to rate the importance of the features he offers, such as taste, size, ingredients, atmosphere and service. You will be surprised how honest people are when you ask how you can improve your service.*

If your business is just starting out, you won't have a lot of customers to ask yet, so "shop" your competition instead. Many retailers routinely drop into their competitors' stores to see what and how they are selling. If you're really brave, try asking a few of the customers after they leave the premises what they like and dislike about the competitors' products and services.

Once you've gone through this three-step market intelligence process, you need to take the next--and hardest--step: clearing your mind of any preconceived ideas about your product or service and being brutally honest. What features of your business jump out at you as something that sets you apart? What can you promote that will make customers want to patronize your business? How can you position your business to highlight your USP?

Don't get discouraged. Successful business ownership is not about having a unique product or service; it's about making your product stand out--even in a market filled with similar items.

Your Unique Value Proposition (UVP)

The primary objective of the LinkedIn™ profile is to articulate your Unique Value Proposition (UVP). You may only get one shot to sell yourself here. Your UVP is "linked" to the quality of your deliverable and to the extent that you can convey your competence, credibility and integrity - in a word, trust.

Subtle inclusions (or deletions) of text, symbols, and media can influence visitors to your LinkedIn™ profile and tip the scales in your favor. You can be creative and indeed a little creativity goes a long way in differentiating yourself, especially if you want to stand out.

Creating Company Profile

https://www.linkedin.com/company/add/show

Type in your company information and email and click on 'Continue' and you will be taken to the next screen.

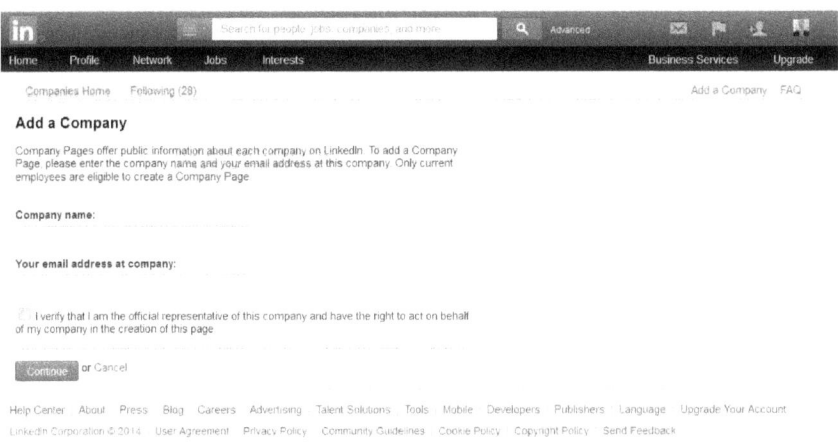

Go to your email account and follow the instructions in the email you have received. It will contain a link that you can click on to verify your company email account.

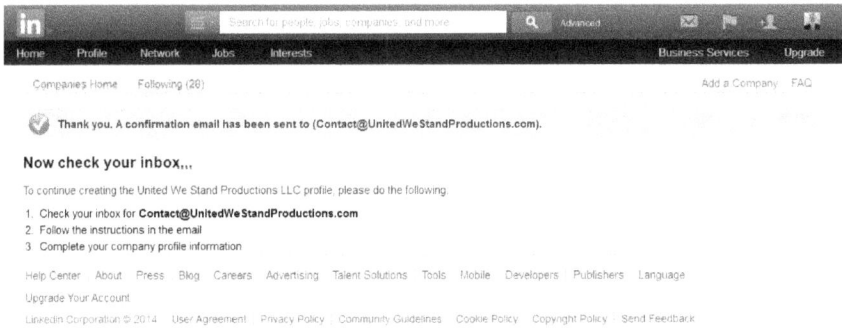

When you click on the link you will be taken back to the following screen where you will complete your company profile.

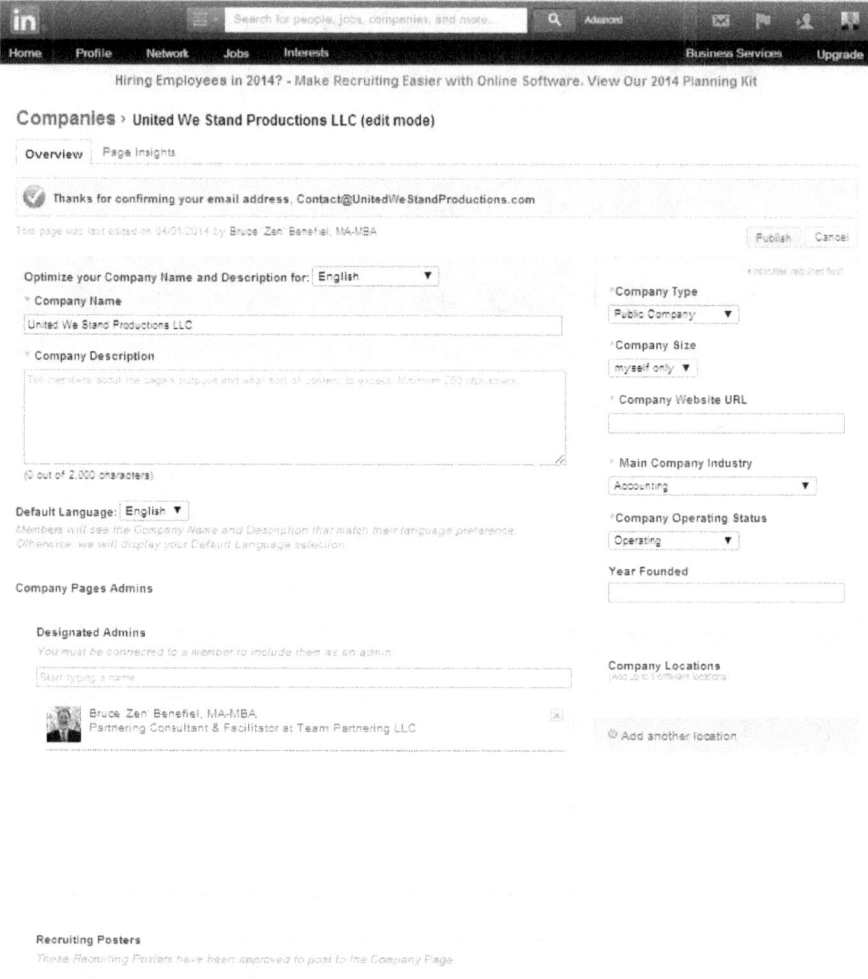

Key Points:

- Dynamic Keywords in Company Description
- Description NOT Sales Copy
- Define Customer and/or Target Market
- Demonstrate Excellence in Products/Services
- Develop Desire

26 Tips: LinkedIn™ Best Practices

Ken Krogue

(Some of the material may be redundant – that means it works!)

LinkedIn™ may be the best source of sales intelligence on the planet for finding and reaching out to a prospective customer.

From our perspective in the inside sales industry, we have found LinkedIn™ has become one of the leading tools inside sales reps use to connect to and meet qualified prospects. In fact, we get so many requests for tips on how to use LinkedIn™ efficiently, we've compiled a sales LinkedIn™ eBook with 42 tips (some the same as listed below, but some new ideas, too) on how to use LinkedIn™ for sales intelligence.

Here is what works:

1- **Use CEO clout through LinkedIn™ to close deals:** Dave Elkington, our CEO, just shared a great technique he learned from Josh James, of Omniture/Adobe fame. Often the CEO or sales executive can reach out to prospective clients and resolve last-minute issues holding up signing a sales agreement. They can push it over the edge. (And I'm writing this on the last day of the quarter. Any of you in sales knows the pressure to finish out a quarter with great results.)

LinkedIn™ helps reach out quickly.

2- **Grab your names:** If you haven't already done this, get on LinkedIn™ and grab your name and your company name. Edit the URL on your profile so it reads with your actual name like this: http://www.LinkedIn.com/in/kenkrogue. If you leave what LinkedIn™ automatically does for you there will be lots of extra numbers and characters which confuse people.

3- **Complete your profile:** Nothing screams "Rookie" like an unfinished profile. Take the time and get it done, both for yourself and your company. There are a few other essentials to getting started. A new book called The

LinkedIn™ Essentials by Asia Bird is helpful, as is the eBook How to Use LinkedIn™ for Business by Hubspot.

4- **Connect to your warm market:** If you can't figure out who to connect with, start with friends, colleagues, and family. The average wedding planner knows that any given person knows about 250 people to invite to a wedding. Make your wedding list. If you are an old timer, make your funeral list.

5- **Use LinkedIn™ to follow up after other communications:** Don't make the mistake of trying to connect with lots people you don't know. LinkedIn™ will warn you, and then shut you down if too many people don't respond to your connection request. Whenever you receive an email, business card, or leave a voicemail; put a "PS" that you are going to also connect by LinkedIn™ right at the end. Then people make the connection as someone they know and approve your connection request.

I also recommend that you change the standard connection request message that LinkedIn™ puts in to something you write that is more personal.

6- **Select your "Doorway" people:** LinkedIn™ lets you see two levels deep of connections for free (and more with the premium version – highly recommended). I'm a Doorway person in my company because I connect to nearly 3000 sales people, managers, and executives. If all my sales reps are connected to me, when I connect to people in companies, they can see them also.

7- **Teach LinkedIn™ strategy and tactics to your employees:** Get your people together and coordinate your efforts and strategies. Years ago, my business partner Dave Elkington, started a company-wide Friday morning meeting where we constantly share new approaches and ideas with each other as part of our culture. We even started a Social Media group of super users who really push the envelope.

8- **Expand your LinkedIn™ reach with Twitter:** There is a little checkbox at the bottom of your "Share an update" box that copies everything you share with your Connections to all of your Twitter followers.

9- **Use your "3 Free Backlinks" with all employees:** Google GOOG -0.5% uses backlinks to drive search engine results. Every LinkedIn™ account has a place for 3 Free Backlinks, and LinkedIn™ leaves these links open to indexing by Google. We have 110 employees, times 3, that's 330 potential backlinks to drive your website up the search engine results list, hmmmmm.

10- **Freely give and receive recommendations:** The Internet is a world of views, likes, shares, and comments. But best of all is a heart-felt recommendation, which you can do on LinkedIn™. Nothing boosts morale, loyalty, and friendship, like an unsolicited recommendation. Try it. And don't be afraid to ask for it from co-workers, friends, and even customers.

11- **Define your offensive sales strategy:** As an old football coach, I know you need both offense and defense. Offense on LinkedIn™ is sales, marketing, and recruiting. Defense is preventing your best employees from being recruited away and your customers stolen by the competition. Everything you learn to do here and elsewhere, recruiters and your competition are learning as well. Keep that in mind when accepting invitations to "connect".

12- **Find doorways to prospects:** Just like you want to focus certain people in your company to be Doorways (lots of connections), there are people at almost every other company who are naturally more connected than others. Connect to those that are highly connected in their own company and they open the doorway for you.

13- **Teach 3×3 analysis to all inside sales people:** Before your sales reps make a call to a prospect, have them spend 3 minutes and find 3 things on LinkedIn™ to talk about. It's much more compelling than talking about the weather. Steve Richard of Vorsight shares this LinkedIn™ technique with clients.

14- **"Test and Invest" in premium services:** I have tested the value of Premium Services on LinkedIn™ (the packages that cost money for Sales, Recruiting, and Job Seekers.) We have found it to be one of the lowest cost, highest return values for lead generation.

15- **Use InMail strategically:** InMail is a great service LinkedIn™ provides where they guarantee a response through a request for introduction, or they give you a credit to use another InMail.

I recently interviewed an industry training consultant by the name of Jamie Shanks, of Sales for Life who uses LinkedIn™ InMail to generate leads for himself and clients for about $20 a lead. He gets a 12% contact to meeting ratio on the first attempt with an increase to a 20% rate with a multi-contact approach.

In a world where Google Adwords leads often cost well over $100 (speaking from experience), LinkedIn™ is proving to be highly effective.

16- **Knock response rates out of the park through LinkedIn™:** At InsideSales.com we constantly test different media through which to send messages to prospects, in addition to testing the content of the messages themselves. In terms of response rates, emails range between .1% and .3%. The exact same message sent by LinkedIn™ in our early in-house tests responded 300% better. Recent tests are much better (but I have to keep a few aces up my sleeve.)

17- **Have sales reps join industry and local LinkedIn™ Groups:** The old days of lunch clubs and breakfast networking groups are being replaced by online groups. I wrote a while back about Trish Bertuzzi, the Founder and CEO of The Bridge Group, in Boston. She formed a LinkedIn™ industry group called Inside Sales Experts. When I first joined there were 8,000 members. I checked today and there are 17,755. I don't know anywhere else on the planet where that many inside sales professionals congregate. Over the years I have now met hundreds of them and I count them as friends. I got involved in their discussions and made friends and acquaintances.

Trish's only rule? No self-promotion.

18- **Use advanced search to target specific titles and industries:** Besides Groups, you can search for the exact title of people and industry of companies that fit your perfect target prospect. The Premium service lets you see many more profiles when you search, and it provides more powerful filters to search by. The Premium service pays for itself in saved labor costs alone.

19- **Follow your customers:** Using the LinkedIn™ company accounts feature, post your own company information, but also follow other companies. Follow your customers. LinkedIn™ ties you into news feeds. It helps you meet the right people to offer a better experience.

20- **Follow your prospects:** Information and sales intelligence often provide "trigger events" that help you know when your prospects may be expanding or growing and thereby needing more of what you sell.

21- **Use "Tags" to categorize your connections:** Tags are like Circles on Google+. They are categories you can use to organize your Contacts or Connections. Add Tags in the Contacts section of LinkedIn™. I use them to differentiate friends, partners, prospects, large prospects, customers, students, press, etc.

22- **Ask for referrals through LinkedIn™:** Salespeople all know that the best way to do business is with referrals. The problem is people can seldom think of someone to refer you to. Now you can spend a few moments in their LinkedIn™ Contact list and find just the right people you want to be referred to. Ask each contact for the referral connection and give the specific names of the contacts you have in mind.

23- **Set up your defense:** In an earlier article I have warned that all of these great tools can also be used against you.

24- **Manage recruiter connections carefully:** If you are a Doorway in your company, be careful who you connect to.

25- **Manage competitor connections carefully:** Ditto!

26- **Never SPAM!** Don't send out mass sales messages by LinkedIn™. This is another word for SPAM. Marketers zealously overused direct mail, the phone, fax, predictive dialer, and email by sending SPAM and driving people nuts. If someone does that to me I actually respond and let them know that only rookie salespeople do that in LinkedIn™.

Just don't do it to others, period.

Here's an excerpt from an article by one of **Hub Spot**'s social media gurus, Sasha Laferte, that explains the new Showcase Pages on LinkedIn™.

A Beginner's Guide to LinkedIn™ Showcase Pages

Having more than one buyer persona is a balancing act. If they're very different, you may feel like you're constantly in danger of not giving one enough attention, or confusing your personas with untargeted content. Add the problem of keeping all your content grouped together on one social media page, and you're really lost.

Some brands have found a way to fix this issue on LinkedIn™, specifically, by creating something called Showcase Pages. Let's take Gap as an example -- they've got a page for Old Navy, Banana Republic, Gap, and Gap Inc. But those pages aren't all connected or centralized around Gap Inc. Showcase Pages, however, fix this problem.

What are Showcase Pages?

Showcase Pages are niche pages off of a company page. They allow a company to promote specific products or market to a specific buyer persona. LinkedIn™ users can follow singular Showcase Pages without following the business or their other Showcase Pages. This allows businesses to promote for and cater to the audience specific to the page.

In other words, if you have a pet boutique, your dog-lover customers won't be subjected to reading about your blog post on the new tank cleaning spray for iguanas. With Showcase Pages, marketers can create hassle-free content that's personalized to the audience they're selling to.

This allows companies to drill down into each of their buyer personas more deeply and keep content personal and interesting. Once that content is published, LinkedIn™ provides businesses with useful, dedicated analytics for each page.

Microsoft, along with Cisco, Intel, and Adobe were among the first to implement Showcase Pages into their marketing strategy. Microsoft has been particularly successful, with Showcase Pages that have upwards of 9,000 followers.

It's important to note that if your business already has more than one Company Page, there's no easy way to move these from Company Pages to Showcase Pages. The LinkedIn™ blog does say, however, that they're exploring the opportunity to have this available in the future. It's also important to note that Showcase Pages can only link back to one centralized Company Page.

Differences Between Showcase Pages and Other LinkedIn™ Pages

Here's what's important to know to differentiate Showcase Pages in your head from the other LinkedIn™ Pages.

- *Showcase Pages have a larger hero image.*
- *They have a two-column newspaper-like layout for content posts.*
- *Unlike Group Pages, businesses can advertise and buy sponsored updates.*
- *Unlike Company Pages, there are no careers, products, or services tabs at the top of the page.*
- *All Showcase Pages link directly back to the business page. This means your pages are all centralized around your company.*
- *Employee profiles cannot be associated with a Showcase Page.*

Exercise:

Boil down the values of your business into a few key words. These can be adjectives such as intelligent, professional, frank or witty. Equally, they can be phrases or non-descriptive words such as love, think, best friend, push yourself.

Look for these around your office – in the emails you send, the posters on walls, notes on the fridge, etc. Asking colleagues for ideas is also likely to turn up an assortment of different types of results, from which you can identify recurring themes.

e.g.

- **Apple:** innovate, inspire, dream.
- **Innocent:** cheeky, fun, everyday.
- **Red Bull:** adventure, try, adrenaline.

Creating a Showcase Page

LinkedIn™ has made some recent changes to the Company Page options. As of April, 2014 LinkedIn™ no longer provides Product/Service Pages. Now there are Showcase Page Listings only. So, with that in mind let us look at the basics. We shared this information earlier, but here it is again:

Here is a list:

1) Standard Company logo – hi-res image 100x60 pixels
2) Square Logo 50x50 pixels
3) 974px by 330px images for your company, products and services
4) Company description that sizzles
5) Product/Service description that sells, but not overtly
6) Unique Selling Proposition – your simply sizzling hook

First of all you will want to go to your company profile page you just created. Next, click on the blue Edit button in the upper right-hand corner. You will see a drop down menu with **Create a Showcase Page** at the bottom of the list. Click on that and you will get this pop up screen:

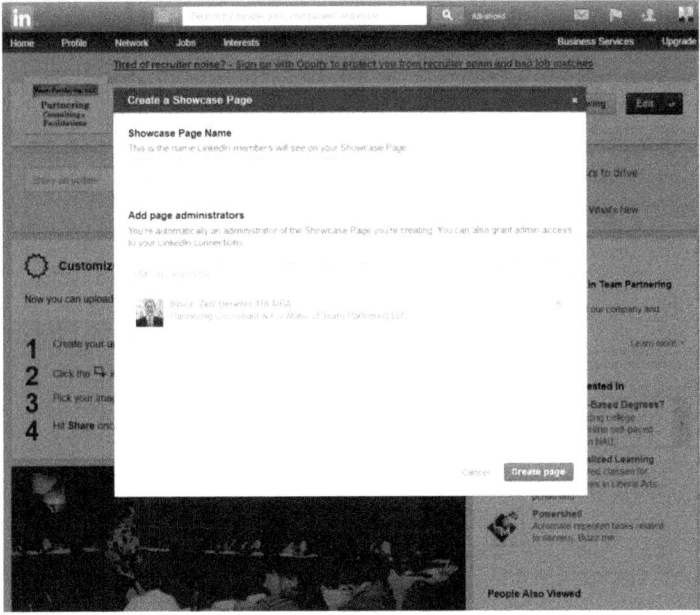

Put your cursor in the blank box under the heading **Showcase Page Name**
and type in the name you want to call the page. Consider how to stand out
with this page title with the stand out keywords you developed earlier.

Example:

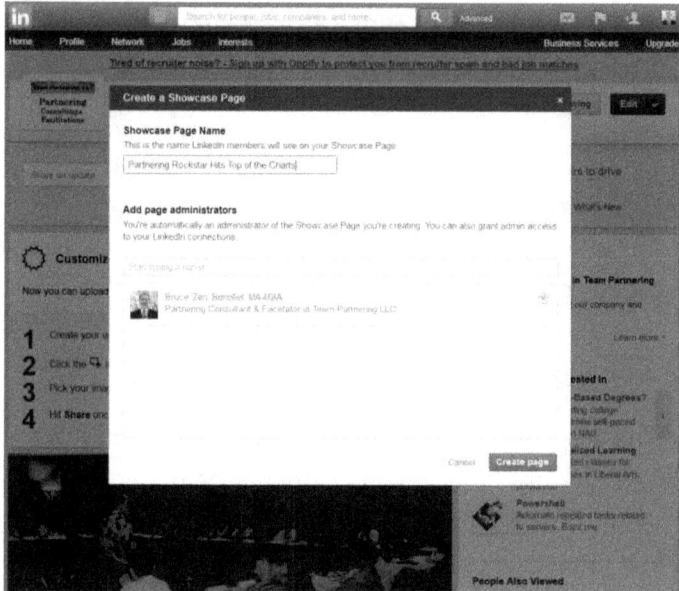

Then you will be taken to this page once the name is saved:

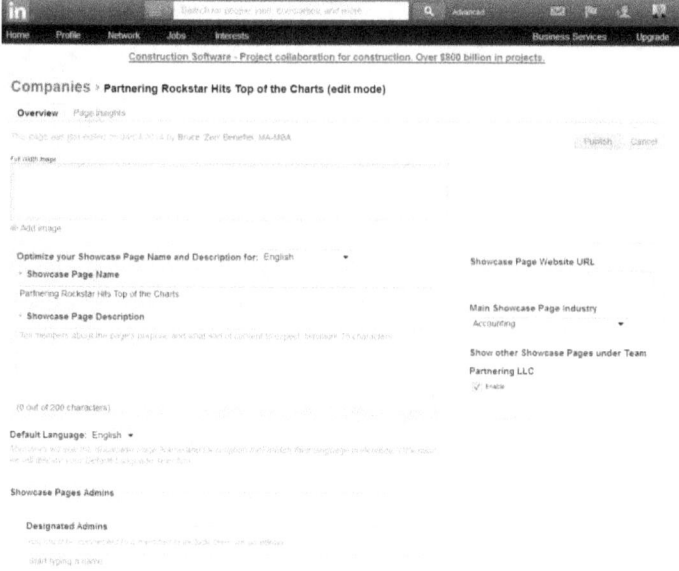

This is where you will add your company image. It should be something stylish that may contain your logo or an image that readily identifies what you do or the products you sell. Just follow the instructions on the page.

This is an opportunity for you to create an outstanding presentation for your company or business. Be creative and even a bit outlandish if you can stretch yourself to do so. In today's market, you've got to stand out before you say a word in presenting your image. Here are examples of some 'outstanding' Showcase Pages.

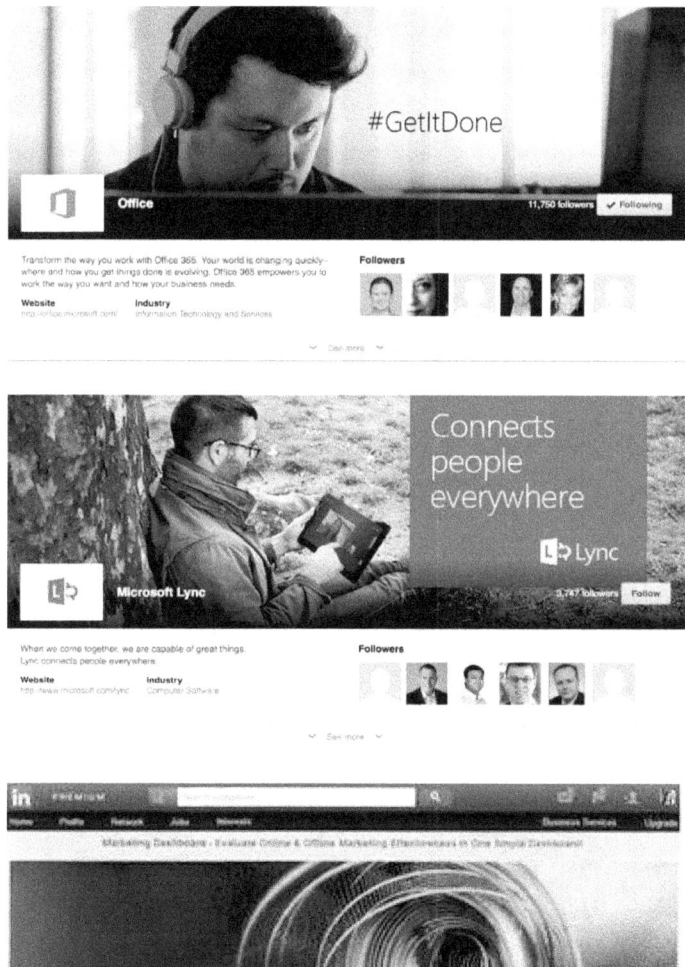

Linked in.
STATISTICS 2013

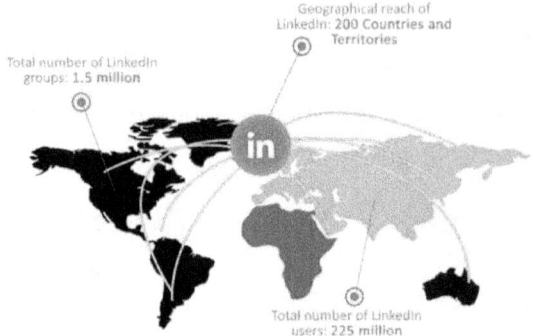

Geographical reach of
LinkedIn: 200 Countries and
Territories

Total number of LinkedIn
groups: 1.5 million

Total number of LinkedIn
users: 225 million

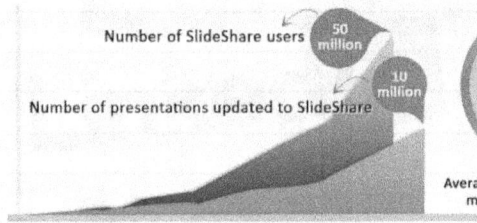

Number of SlideShare users — 50 million

Number of presentations updated to SlideShare — 10 million

17 MINUTES

Average time a user spends
monthly on LinkedIn

27%

Percentage of LinkedIn
visits via mobile

5

Average number of
endorsements per LinkedIn user

2.7million

Total number of LinkedIn
business pages

$119 million
Amount LinkedIn spent on
purchasing SlideShare

1 billion
Total number of LinkedIn
endorsements

3,700
Total number of LinkedIn employees

75,000
Total number of developers using LinkedIn's API

submitedge
www.submitedge.com

Source for #LinkedIn Statistics:
Expanded Ramblings

Search Engine Optimization | Social Media Optimization

Building Your Network

First, make sure you have taken advantage of the import features in LinkedIn™ for your email contacts. Hover you cursor on the Network link in the menu bar just below the search bar in the middle of the top of the LinkedIn™ screen. You will get a drop down menu, then click on "Add Connections" and you will see this screen:

You can import your contacts from this page. Your email will automatically appear in the 'Your email' box. If you have Gmail contacts you want to import, click on the Gmail Icon and click 'Continue.' You will get something that looks like this:

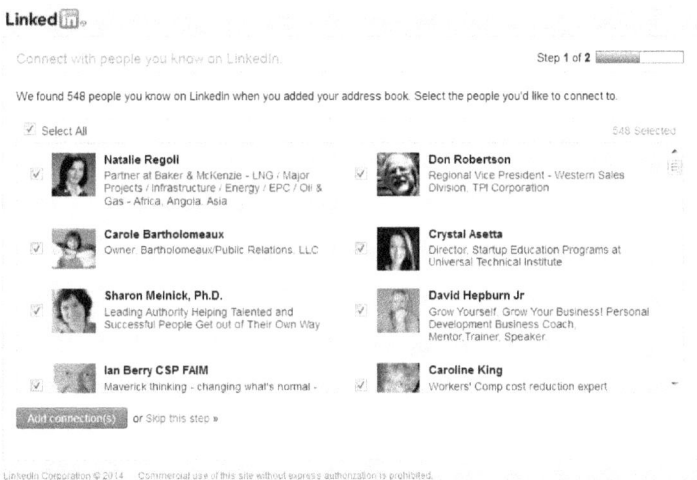

If you are using Outlook as an individual and not from a company server, you won't be able to import them here. You can, however you can load a CSV file from Outlook after you save your contacts. For now, the when you click 'Add Connections' from the page you'll get something like this:

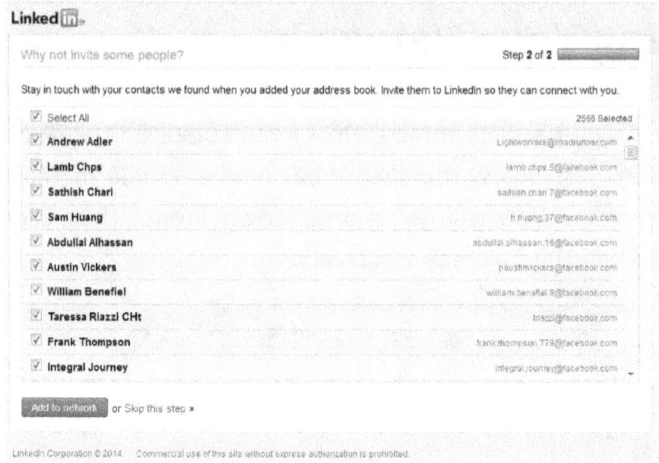

You can add all of these contacts or select which ones you want. Then you do the same for each of the other email services, if you use them. That is the basic and simple method. There are other options if you click on 'Contacts' and then on the GEAR icon you will get this:

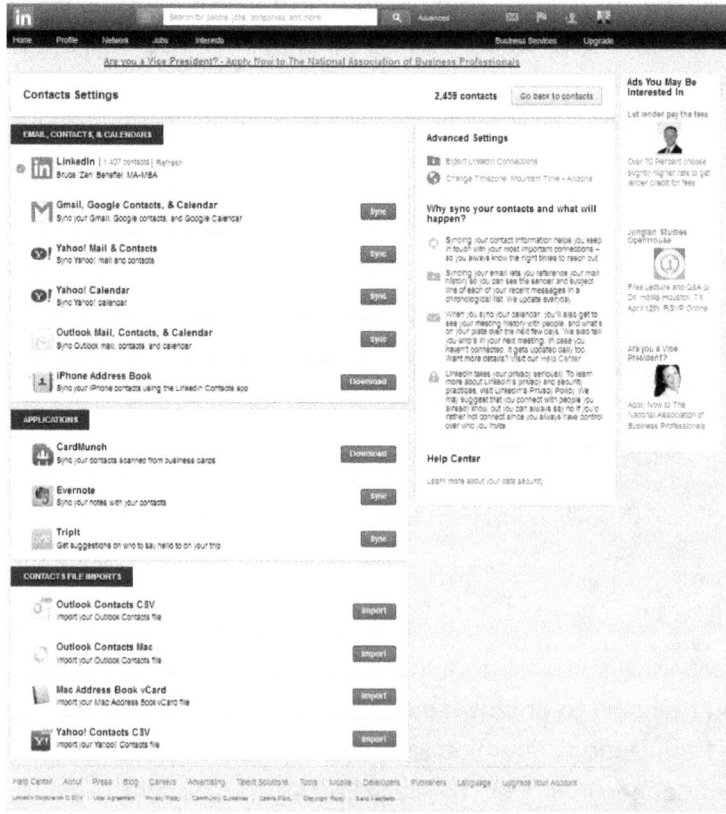

Once you have those in and/or have an established contact base, then you can begin to go hunting for the perfect game... your potential clients or customers. Now for some cool stuff you can do from your contacts. On the screen you were just on, look in the upper right for the **Advanced Settings**. Just below it you will see **Export LinkedIn™ Connections**.

Guess what you can do with this? Yes, you can download a .CSV file and import it into Outlook so you can use it with a Mail Merge program and email your entire list.

LinkedIn™ Built-in CRM

One of most brilliant aspects of this platform is its built-in CRM feature. You can access it several ways. Probably the first step is to go through your existing contacts and 'Tag' them appropriately. You can tag them any way you would like, preferably in your market segments first. This will be critical when you begin to market to your prospects.

Go to your Contacts page and 'mouse over' your contact's information to the right of their picture. Notice that after each one there are three links that appear just below their information as you pull your cursor down. Those links are: 'tag,' 'message' and 'more.' Click on the 'tag' link to create a new tag or click the box of the tag(s) you have already created.

Once done, when you go to your Contacts page in the future you can sort them by tag. There are other sorting options as well. The built-in CRM has other functions you can access from the Contact's profile as well. Those are available under the Contact's profile image. You will see two items:

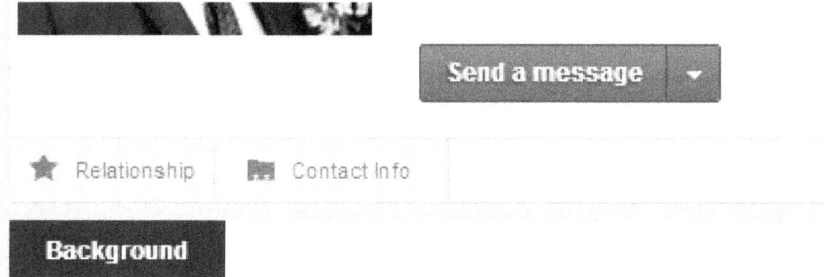

Relationship & Contact Info Tabs

When the 'Relationship' tab is selected you will see the four items above. This feature allows you to keep track of virtually all your information on each contact or prospective client/customer.

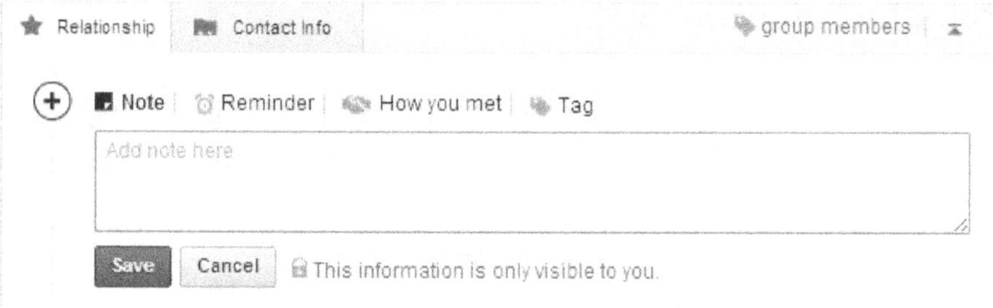

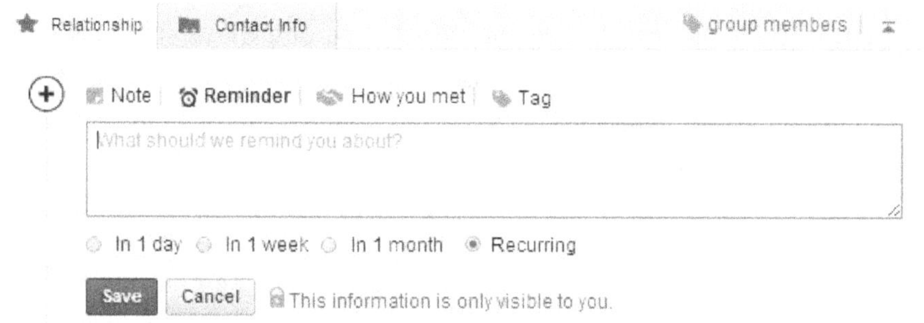

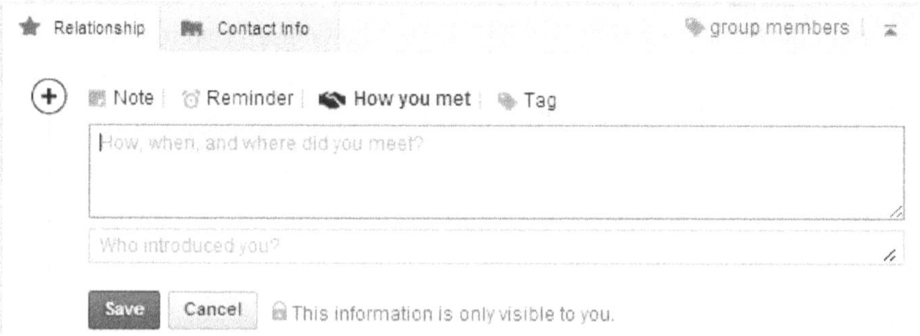

Some interesting data:

Like this infographic? You'll ♥ my classes: http://socialmediaonlineclasses.com

Linked in
Networking Strategies

PROFILE
1 Use headshot photo, not logo
2 Write headline with keywords
3 Claim your custom LI URL
4 Add multimedia to Gallery
5 Get 2+ recommendations
6 Connect w/people who view your profile
7 Add links for calls-to-action
8 Customize contact info w/ CTA

COMPANY PAGE
9 Build robust company page
10 Add your products/services
11 Add video for each product
12 Include deep descriptions
13 Get recommendations for each product/service
14 Post updates from company
15 Link to product pages
16 Mine insights for follower info

SEARCH
17 Search for sales leads
18 Find college alumni
19 Search employees by company
20 Filter results geographically
21 Save searches & have LI email results weekly
22 Save up to 3 searches
23 Search Groups & Companies
24 Search for jobs by industry

RECOMMENDATIONS
57 Recs set you apart as trustworthy
58 Ask for recs from clients
59 Provide recs consistently
60 Be specific when providing
61 Only LI users can provide recs
62 Strengthens client relationships
63 Create system of asking for recs
64 Provides details missing from endorsements

GALLERY
25 Include multimedia on profile page
26 Any section can have a gallery
27 Add photos, videos, PDFs
28 Insert links in gallery descriptions
29 Create 30 sec welcome video for LI
30 Write actionable gallery titles
31 Include CTA links in descriptions
32 Send to landing page for optin

ENDORSEMENTS
49 Once-click credibility
50 Add skills to your profile first
51 News Feed shows latest
52 No opportunity for detail
53 Email notifications for new
54 Endorse top colleagues
55 Endorse wisely, ethically
56 Recommendations allow detail, endorsements is quick, lite

CONNECTIONS
41 Quality connections paramount
42 Start w/colleagues, alumni
43 Expand to clients, vendors
44 Include past employers
45 Add mentors, professors
46 Invite leads found via search
47 Connect w/ industry experts
48 Identify superconnectors

GROUPS
33 #1 Rule: Engage, don't broadcast
34 Ask colleagues for groups they use
35 Review group content before joining
36 Are connections group members?
37 Introduce yourself once joined
38 Initiate & participate in discussions
39 Increase visibility to LI & traffic to your website
40 Great place to ask questions

@SM_OnlineClass
facebook.com/socialmediaonlineclasses

SocialMedia
OnlineClasses.com

Getting Leads from LinkedIn™

First of all, let us explore the Advanced link right next to the search bar at the top of the page. You will see it right next to the blue magnifying glass. There are many options as to how to search for the initial contacts that you may need in an organization.

The options are quite extensive. In this version (free) of LinkedIn™ you will be able to look through your 1st and 2nd tier connections, Group Members and 3rd tier members with everyone else as separate searches. If you close that window, you will see your 1st, 2nd and Group Members

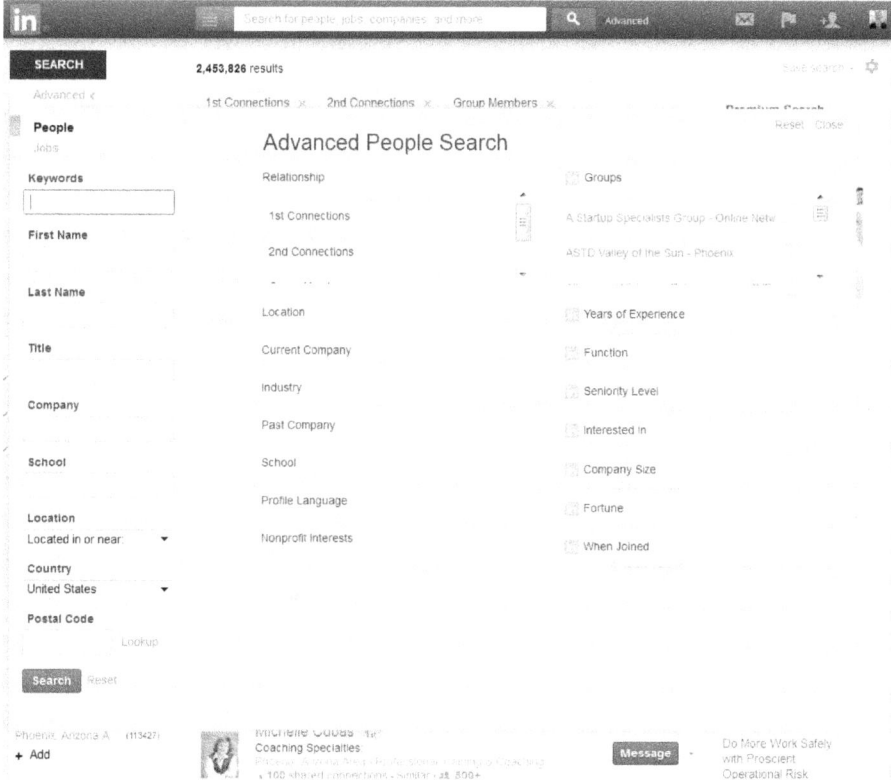

Now that this is open, what do you think you need to do? Look around at the various options you have for which to perform your search. If you haven't already, once you do your search you can 'tag' specific ones for further development in your sales funnel.

10 Best Email Practices

What about email marketing? Everyone uses it, but do they use it effectively? How do you?

The infographic to the left was delivered to me recently, as I was compiling the information for this book. I find it very interesting that when you are focused on something you enjoy and that ultimately benefits others, the synchronicity of things showing up just amazes me.

This brings up an important and tasty tidbit of awareness that I strongly suggest you incorporate in your daily deliberations... gratitude! Be thankful for everything you have and receive.

This business of marketing and sales is more of an exercise in social architecture; moving people, places and things into an appropriate order so that products and/or services align with needs and rewards are commensurate. It is a process.

Developing Relationships

Sales is a higher form of communication indeed, as Allan Himmelstein with SalesCoachAZ.com states. In that higher form of communication there are noticeable differences in the high performers. Are you one?

We will highlight some key points in developing relationships through LinkedIn™ that will support the higher form of communication and best practices in electronic conversations. Electronic communication, the written word, is extremely important in developing online relationships that lead to accessing decision-makers and closing deals.

Referring back to the sales statistics from earlier, the majority of sales happen between the 5th and 12th touches. Start with that in mind. You are not in a sprint. You are in a marathon. Train to win. Show you care.

Here is a list of some best practices: (options to consider)

1) Study your contact list for the markets you wish to explore.
2) Compile a list of potential decision-makers and/or gatekeepers.
3) Determine the best candidates and closeness (within your 3 degrees) of decision-makers. Ask for introductions if necessary.
4) Craft a re-introduction to your personal 1st line contacts that is open and personal. Do NOT ask any closing questions. Ask them if they would be open to further communication... FOLLOW UP!
5) **Do pertinent research on the companies and their leadership.**
6) Ask for introductions to the company decision-makers. Sometimes these are available through other lists and/or company pages.
7) Craft an appropriate introduction via a personal note. **DO NOT EVER USE THE DEFAULT LINKEDIN™ MESSAGE**
8) Ask the decision-maker questions about **their needs** and invite them to respond or ask them if they would be open to a short survey because you respect their attention and time availability.
9) Prepare a survey of needs that you can deliver via a link to their inbox. Online tools such as *Survey Monkey* are useful (and free). This will give you an opportunity to demonstrate your industry knowledge by the types of questions you ask.
10) Ask for a phone conversation or face-to-face to discuss results.

There are certainly other options that were not included in the list. You may have your own best practices, but just need help in getting to the decision-makers through the use of LinkedIn™. We trust that the information we have provided with assist you in that effort.

Here is an article on the same subject that was published on INC.com:

10 Ways to Generate More Leads and Referrals on LinkedIn™
BY JEFF HADEN @JEFF_HADEN (from Inc.com)

It's not hard--and may be the best 20 minutes you spend every day. Everyone seems to be on LinkedIn™. So you are too. But are you actually generating leads and referrals?

Here's a blueprint for using LinkedIn™ to prospect more effectively from Sandler Training, a leading sales, management, and leadership training organization.

1. Prepare a digital version of your 30-Second Commercial and include that text in your LinkedIn™ profile. The main thing to remember about LinkedIn™ is this: It is a huge, never-ending, virtual networking event, and you have to be ready with the right response to, "What do you do?"

Your 30-second commercial is the answer to that question, as told from the point of view of a *prospect in pain* that eventually *turned into your happy customer*.

For instance: "We specialize in custom designed inventory management systems for manufacturing and distribution operations. We've been particularly successful with companies in the X, Y, and Z industries that are concerned about the costs associated with inaccurate inventory counts, unhappy with frequent paperwork bottlenecks that slow down the fulfillment process, or disappointed by the amount of time it takes to reconcile purchasing, invoicing, and shipping records. We've been able to create hand-in-glove inventory management systems that help our customers save time, attention, and money."

If something like this isn't on your LinkedIn™ profile you're at a competitive disadvantage.

2. Add connections to your network. If you invest a minute or so each working day clicking the "connect" button on the "People You May Know" list that LinkedIn™ posts in your feed you will broaden your network, and you will become known as someone who broadens the network, which is just as important.

Remember: Everyone you talk to about business or meet during the course of the business day is a potential LinkedIn™ connection.

3. Play fair. But only "connect" to people you actually know. LinkedIn™ will backfire on you if you pretend to know people you don't. (While we're at it, here are nine other mistakes people make on LinkedIn™.)

Always ask for introductions to people you don't know.

4. Build out your lead list. Spend five minutes a day investigating the connections of your contacts to see whom you don't know personally but would like to meet. Make a note of those to whom you would like introductions. Start first with the "Recommendations," since those are most likely the strongest relationships of the LinkedIn™ user you are viewing.

Ask for the recommendations outside of your LinkedIn™ account via email or phone. You'll get a quicker answer. (And you'll get the chance to quickly reconnect with your connections.)

5. Follow your current clients and prospects. Spend another two minutes each day looking up your current clients and top prospects. Find out whether they have a company page. If they do, follow and monitor it.

6. Post an update. Spend 60 seconds each working day posting an "Update" to your LinkedIn™ network. Use the daily update to share a link to an article or a video that is relevant to your prospects and customers. Or use the "Pulse" (used to be known as "LinkedIn™ Today") feature on your LinkedIn™ dashboard.

Each time you post an update you get displayed on the feed of all the people with whom you are connected. But never sell when you post updates. Add value and share expertise instead.

7. Join groups. LinkedIn™ lets you connect with people who are in groups with you. Use this as a targeted way to add value to others, share insights, and build out your network with prospects. Invest five minutes a day on this. (Here are tips to find the best groups to join.)

8. Use LinkedIn™ to celebrate the accomplishments of others. When you come across a news story or post that offers good news about your client or prospect, or any key contact, share the news as a status update. Recognize the person with an "@" reply. That will ensure they receive notification of the mention. Spend a minute a day on this.

9. Write a recommendation. It is often difficult to secure LinkedIn™ recommendations, if only because it takes the writer time to log in, write, and post them.

Instead of waiting for someone to recommend you, devote five minutes a day to writing and posting (reality-based) recommendations for your customers and key contacts. Once your contact approves the text, the recommendation will show up on his/her LinkedIn™ account.

This will align you with your contact, serve as a permanent top-of-mind promotional piece for you and your organization, show your network that you work together, and make it much more likely that your contact will look for a way return the favor. That could be either a referral or a recommendation.

Often, it's both.

10. Stop. The key to success on LinkedIn™ is investing a little bit of time every working day--not six hours a day for a week straight, then nothing.

Do all of this regularly. The maximum total time investment should be 20 minutes a day, not including developing your 30-Second Commercial (which you should finish before you even log into LinkedIn™.)

Invest that twenty minutes a day, consistently, for thirty straight working days, and you will start generating more prospects and referrals from LinkedIn™. Then... *keep it up!*

11 Tips to Find the Best LinkedIn™ Groups

by Jeff Haden (from Inc.com)

A friend of mine landed his last six clients as a direct result of his participation in LinkedIn Groups. Another sees his groups as a natural extension of his social-media marketing efforts.

And believe it or not (I still find it hard to believe), a third somehow managed to meet her fiancé in an HR-focused group.

LinkedIn groups are informal communities formed around industries, professions, themes, niche topics, etc. Because any LinkedIn member can create one, there are now well over a million groups.

Find and join the right groups, and it's easy to keep up with news and trends, make connections, ask and answer questions, land new clients-- even start a romance. (Well, maybe that last one isn't so easy.)

Here's how to find the right groups for you:

Set your goals.

Because groups are relatively focused, one group probably can't meet all your needs. Decide whether you're looking to connect with potential clients, establish your credentials and authority, learn more about your field--determine what you hope to achieve.

If you're new to groups, start with one primary goal. You can always branch out later.

Then search.

Go to the Groups Directory page and enter search terms related to your goal.

Just keep in mind that searching broad terms will generate broad results; search *marketing,* and you get more than 41,000 results; *social-media marketing* yields more than 4,000 results. Think about what you're looking for and use search terms that are as specific as possible.

And sift.

You can refine your search by using the check boxes on the left-hand side of the page. One handy move is to sift search results by your current connections. For example, you can choose to see only groups that your first and/or second connections have joined.

In some ways, that's handy, but given that most people hope to make new connections by joining groups, don't limit yourself to groups where you already "know someone."

And borrow ideas.

Searching is useful, but so is following the lead of people you respect. Go to any profile page and check out the groups that person belongs to; chances are one or two match your goals.

Plus, joining the same groups increases your chances of connecting with the people you hope to connect with. Chances are, influential people in your industry are members of useful groups, so why not hang out where they hang out?

Then sift through the results.

A search result lists groups in descending order according to the number of members. Under each group is a brief description.

Sometimes the description is helpful. Sometimes, though, the group has veered away from its description and original purpose. The only way to know is to...

Join a few groups.

Pick a few groups that appear to meet your goals--and seem interesting--and join. You can be a member of up to 50 groups, and you can leave a group at any time, so there's no harm in experimenting.

Read recent discussions and click the Members link to find out who else is in the group. If you find heavy hitters or people you respect, that's a good sign.

Keep in mind, some groups are members only; the manager of the group must accept you before you can participate or view discussions. Members-only groups tend to be more focused, but there are plenty of open groups that stay just as on topic and spam free.

Pause and reflect.

Check out the quality of the discussions or updates. Are article or resource references relevant and valuable? Are the discussions interesting? Are there enough members to create a vibrant group?

Think about your goal, and determine if the group is likely to help you reach that goal--and keep in mind you can always leave if your initial impression turns out to be wrong.

Then chill for a bit.

No one likes the guy who walks up and takes over a conversation at a party. Watch, listen, and get a feel for how the group operates. Then gradually start to participate. Start by responding to questions or topics raised by other people. Get a real feel for the group, and let the group get a feel for you, before you start driving discussions.

Otherwise, you're *that* guy, and no one likes that guy.

Stay reasonably active.

You don't need to participate every day, but you should be somewhat regular--otherwise, why are you joining the group?

That's especially true if you hope to establish yourself as an authority; it's hard to spark great discussions and answer questions when you're never there.

Stay small.

Sometimes people will invite you to join a group. Sometimes you'll stumble across a group and think, Why not? Before long, you'll belong to dozens of groups.

It's impossible to participate in a meaningful way in more than a few groups. If you aren't getting the results you want--given the goals you established--don't add more groups to your collection. Find a few groups that better suit your need, and leave the groups that don't.

Besides, no one is impressed by a seemingly endless list of groups on a profile page.

Eventually, consider starting a group.

Anyone can found a group. If your group becomes popular, you can drive traffic to your website and send free weekly messages to group members-- all of whom opted in to receive those messages.

But wait until you really understand how groups operate before you found a group, and think about how you can differentiate your group from the thousands of similar groups that exist.

Otherwise, you may belong to a group of one. But, hey, at least you'll always enjoy the discussions.

Another LinkedIn™ Group Consideration
Excerpt from John Nemo for Social Media Examiner

> LinkedIn allows you to join up to 50 groups. I suggest joining as many as you can for your particular niche or industry. A great perk of being in groups is that you can filter the membership list to find influencers and prospects based on different criteria.
>
> After you've joined a group, go to its Members page. See that list of group members? You can run a filtered search and instantly create a list of ready-made prospects based on specific job titles, company names, physical locations or any other criteria you want to sort by.
>
> One of the biggest mistakes I still see people making on LinkedIn is not taking the time to send a personalized invitation.
>
> Relying on the generic "I'd like to add you to my professional network" message isn't just lazy and ineffective, it can get you blocked or flagged as a spammer which restricts your ability to send invites in the future.

An effective LinkedIn invitation is personalized and clear. Start out with a personal sentence or two, and then explain why you want to connect, how you found the person and the value you bring to the person as a connection.

Here's what I like to do. When I find someone I want to connect with, I open his or her profile in a new tab and scan it for something personal to mention in my invitation. Where did they go to college? Where do they live? Do they have any hobbies or volunteer organizations or causes listed?

A mistake some people make is joining groups, and then taking the spray-and-pray approach. Their interactions and contributions are only sales-related. A more effective approach is reverse engineering.

For example, let's say you want to sell video marketing services to small business owners and you've joined several LinkedIn groups where they hang out. Instead of coming in with the hard sell, write and share a post on a topic of interest to them that highlights your expertise.

In this case, you could write an article explaining how video marketing helps small businesses create trust. Use a compelling title, cite case studies that illustrate your point and end with a call to action encouraging others to share links to their own video marketing clips in the comments—then share one of your own to get the ball rolling.

That type of post does two important things. First, it positions you as an expert on the topic—someone people will want to follow and pay attention to as a trusted resource.

Second, it drums up business. When a group member reads your post and sees your work, they may think, "This guy makes a good point and knows his stuff. Plus, I loved his example in the comments. I wonder what I can do to work with him?"

Another option is to start your post with an open-ended question: "Does your small business use video in its marketing efforts? Why or why not?"

Your post still shares the value mentioned above, but the approach is softer and may entice people to respond and engage with your direct question.

A third option is to look for opportunities to share your wisdom. When another member posts, respond with an insightful comment. This is an effective way to find and engage with people who are looking for the product, service or expertise you have to offer.

Final Thoughts

LinkedIn offers you a treasure trove of personal and professional information about your ideal prospects. Take advantage of it! Use it to personalize your connection and engagement with potential buyers.

Leverage your knowledge, approach and personality in all of your LinkedIn interactions. Remember, the only thing that truly separates you from everyone else who offers similar services or products is YOU!

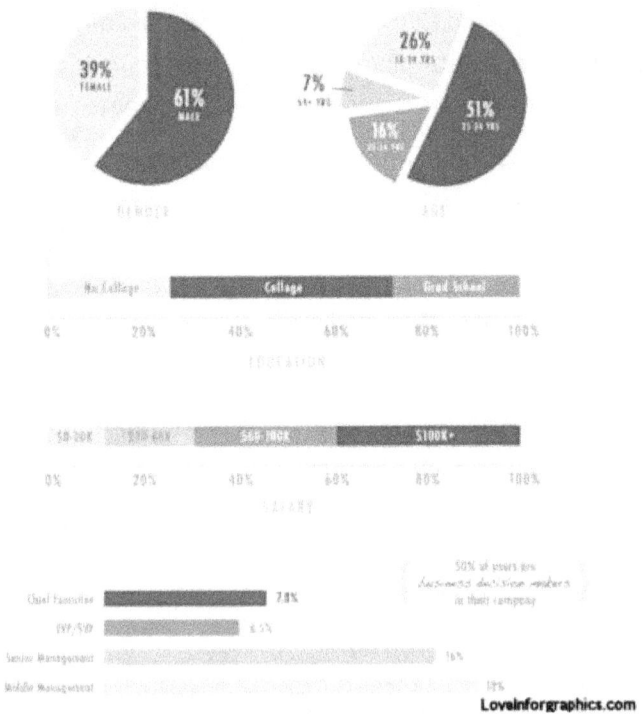

Loveinforgraphics.com

How to Create a Buzz

Now that you have a showcase page you will need to create a buzz with it. What does that mean? Well, you've got to share it far and wide. There are many ways of accomplishing that and we will explore a few of them.

There are no doubt a plethora of choices for your social media needs, some free and some not. Let's look at the free ones for now so that you can get started without being out of pocket... much. We suggest that you do spend a little bit, but it won't cost you an arm and a leg.

Hootsuite.com is a dynamic and feature-filled Pro Plan service that is only $8.99 a month. You can sign up for a free 30-day trial using this link: http://www.kqzyfj.com/click-7405895-10920306. Go ahead and type it into your browser right now. Make sure you type it in the address bar on your browser correctly. You will get the screen below if you did.

 Schedule Posts

Save time by scheduling 100's of messages and launching multiple campaigns at once

 Multiple Networks

Monitor and manage up to 100 Social Profiles such as Twitter, Facebook, Linkedin and Google + Pages from one web-based dashboard.

 Measure

Measure your social media campaigns and track performance with custom social analytics reports.

Over 7 million users and the world's top brands trust HootSuite

Hootsuite allows you create tweets (140 characters including link) and/or longer content messages for LinkedIn™ or Facebook posts.

Once you create your account you'll be able to do some amazing things in minutes that used to take you hours. For now, take a few moments and just explore this feature-filled website and see what is available.

Here is just one example of the capability of this website. You will notice Twitter, Facebook and LinkedIn™ Accounts and Pages listed. You can add multiple profiles, pages and more to this robust suite of Hoots.

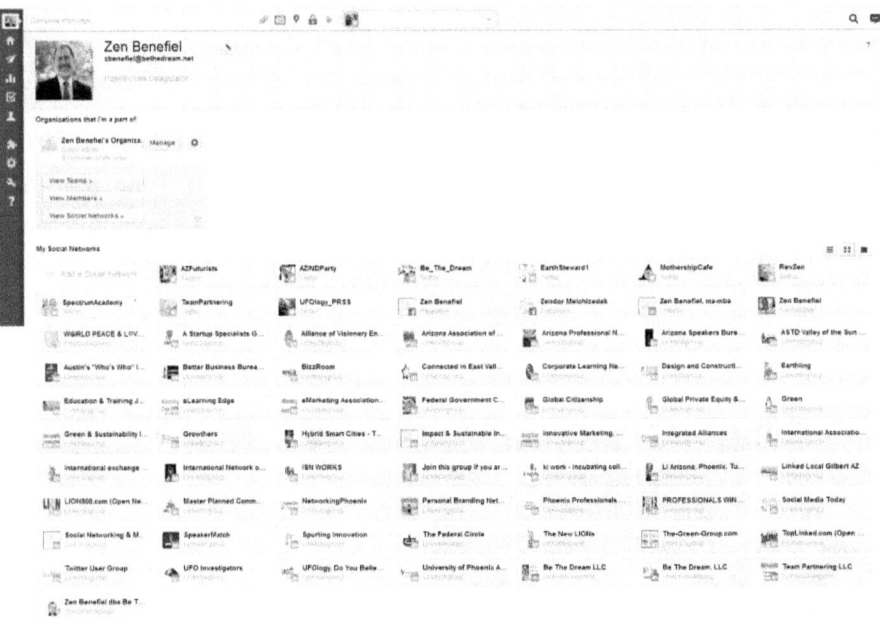

Hootsuite allows you to load up to 50 individual messages and store up to 350 individual messages at once. What a time saver for the avid marketer. If you choose to explore the website further you will find more features that you will know what to do with for a while. Have fun with it.

Pardon the sidebar, but to digress just a moment and relay some addition information about Hootsuite. Among the other features you will have at your disposal is an easy way to keep track of who is connected with you on Twitter and you can follow or unfollow right from the Hootsuite panel.

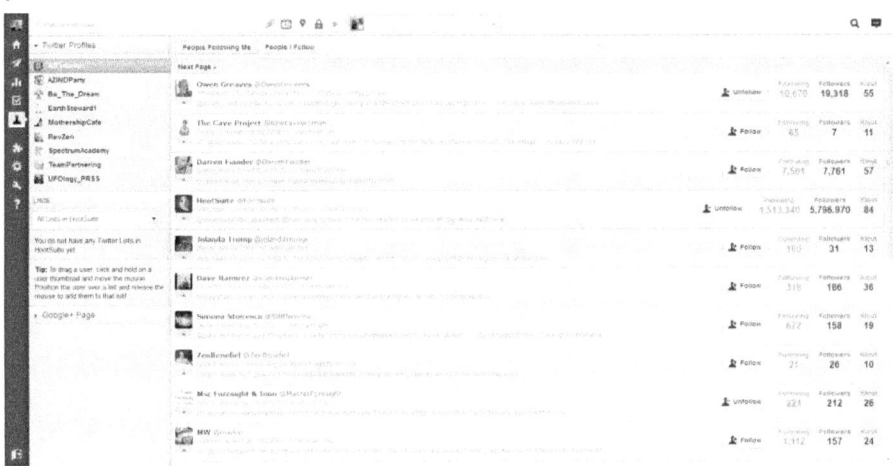

Notice you can follow or unfollow and it contains each followers Klout score as well. Speaking of connecting, you will have some options at the end of this workbook.

The B2B Tool Set to Transform your Business

 # LinkedIn Marketing

AN EVER GROWING MARKET OF POTENTIAL LEADS

OVER 200 MILLION ACTIVE USERS AROUND THE WORLD IN 2013

THE UK HAS 11 MILLION LINKEDIN MEMBERS. ONLY THE USA AND INDIA HAVE MORE MEMBERS

IT TOOK 6 YEARS FOR LINKEDIN TO REACH 50 MILLION USERS

LINKEDIN ADDED 50 MILLION MEMBERS IN 2011 ALONE

USERS ARE JOINING LINKEDIN AT A RATE OF 2 MEMBERS PER SECOND

OVER 25 MILLION LINKEDIN PROFILES ARE VIEWED EVERY DAY

OVER 175,000 NEW LINKEDIN PROFILES CREATED EVERY DAY IN 2012

5 BILLION PROFESSIONAL SEARCHES ON LINKEDIN IN 2012

REACH B2B PROFESSIONALS

80

80% OF USERS ON LINKEDIN INFLUENCE BUSINESS DECISIONS AT THEIR COMPANY

95

95% OF LINKEDIN MEMBERS ARE DEGREE EDUCATED

70k

AVERAGE ANNUAL HOUSEHOLD INCOME FOR A LINKEDIN MEMBER IS AROUND £70,000

£££

BUILD YOUR NETWORK + ENHANCE YOUR PRESENCE

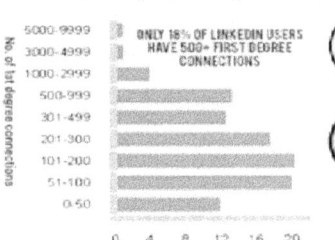

ONLY 18% OF LINKEDIN USERS HAVE 500+ FIRST DEGREE CONNECTIONS

26% OF FORTUNE 500 CEOS ARE ON LINKEDIN. ONLY 8% ARE ON FACEBOOK AND 4% ON TWITTER

90% OF COMPANIES DO NOT DISPLAY THEIR PRODUCTS OR SERVICES ON THEIR LINKEDIN COMPANY PAGE

1 IN 2 LINKEDIN PROFILES ARE INCOMPLETE

GENERATE LEADS AND SALES

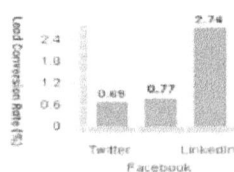

2.74

0.69   0.77

Twitter   LinkedIn
Facebook

82% OF CONSUMERS TRUST INFORMATION FROM LINKEDIN, COMPARED TO JUST 28% FOR TWITTER AND 23% FOR FACEBOOK

ONLY 28% OF COMPANIES ON LINKEDIN USE THE SITE TO IDENTIFY BUSINESS OPPORTUNITIES

LINKEDIN'S LEAD CONVERSION RATE OF 2.74% IS HIGHER THAN THE REST OF THE SOCIAL MEDIA CHANNELS COMBINED

LINKEDIN IS 277% MORE EFFECTIVE FOR LEAD GENERATION THAN FACEBOOK AND TWITTER

INFOGRAPHIC GENERATED BY ONLINE MARKETING AGENCY ONLY WEB

only web

Social Media Impact and Scoring Tools

KLOUT

Klout.com is another social media ranking tool that uses a choice of logins with Twitter, Facebook or your email address. It scores you based on the amount of activity you have in a variety of social networks. The Klout Score is a number between 1-100 that represents your influence. The more influential you are, the higher your Klout Score.

Klout started out as a measurement and ranking tool that is integrated with LinkedIn™, Facebook and Twitter and now has its own features as a social media generator and tracker. You can create, schedule and measure results of your posts across several platforms.

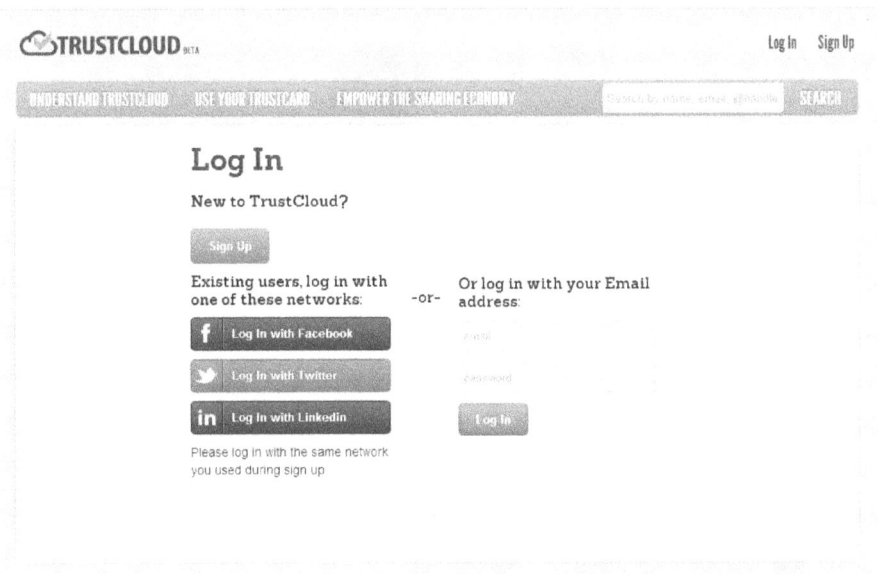

TrustCloud.com goes even deeper into your social media behavior. Of course if you are only using LinkedIn™, then it would probably not do you much good. However, as the marketing world has expanded into a vast array of social media venues, then it might be good to offer a pre-qualifying statement that you are cool, connected and know what you are doing.

TrustCloud is still in its Beta stage, but it is rapidly making an impact.

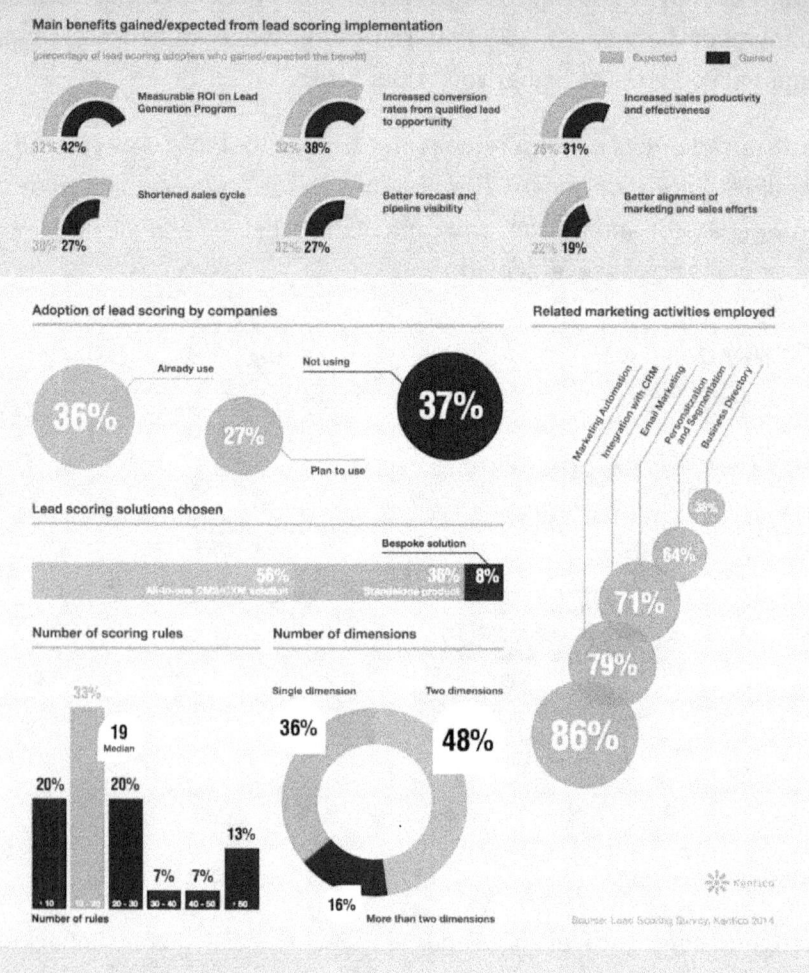

HOW CAN
LEAD SCORING
HELP MY BUSINESS?

Lead scoring enables website owners to classify their visitors according to how likely they are to become customers. Visitors are automatically scored on their website behavior and submitted data using a points system set up to reflect the specific business.

Main benefits gained/expected from lead scoring implementation

(percentage of lead scoring adopters who gained/expected the benefit)

Expected ☐ Gained ■

Measurable ROI on Lead Generation Program — 32% / **42%**

Increased conversion rates from qualified lead to opportunity — 32% / **38%**

Increased sales productivity and effectiveness — 25% / **31%**

Shortened sales cycle — 30% / **27%**

Better forecast and pipeline visibility — 32% / **27%**

Better alignment of marketing and sales efforts — 32% / **19%**

Adoption of lead scoring by companies

Already use **36%**

Plan to use **27%**

Not using **37%**

Related marketing activities employed

- Marketing Automation — 86%
- Integration with CRM — 79%
- Email Marketing — 71%
- Personalization and Segmentation — 64%
- Business Directory — 58%

Lead scoring solutions chosen

All-in-one CMS/CXM solution **56%** | Standalone product **36%** | Bespoke solution **8%**

Number of scoring rules

- < 10: 20%
- 10 - 20: 33%
- 20 - 30: 20%
- 30 - 40: 7%
- 40 - 50: 7%
- > 50: 13%

19 Median

Number of rules

Number of dimensions

Single dimension **36%**

Two dimensions **48%**

More than two dimensions **16%**

Kentico

Source: Lead Scoring Survey, Kentico 2014

56

Some Sales Information

Although you may already know a lot about sales, sometimes it is good to have a little refresher on the importance of certain things. Be comfortable in knowing that getting the gold takes a little time. If you expect immediate results, you'll probably get really frustrated. Consider the same with using the LinkedIn™ resource.

Sales Statistics

- 48% of Sales people never follow up

- 25% of Sales people make a 2nd touch

- 12% of Sales people make 3 touches and quit

- 10% of Sales people make more than 3 touches

- 2% of Sales are made on the 1st touch

- 3% of Sales are made on the 2nd touch

- 5% of Sales are made on the 3rd touch

- 10% of Sales are made on the 4th touch

- 80% of Sales are made on the 5th-12th touch

Customer Statistics

Why do customers leave?

- 1% will die
- 3% will move away
- 5% will buy from a friend
- 9% will buy from a competitor
- 14% will buy from another for product price
- 68% will leave due to perceived indifference

What about continued relationships?

- Repeat customers spend 33% more than new
- Referrals from repeat customers are 107% greater
- Cost 6 times as much to sell to new customers

Here are some ideas for crafting your messages:

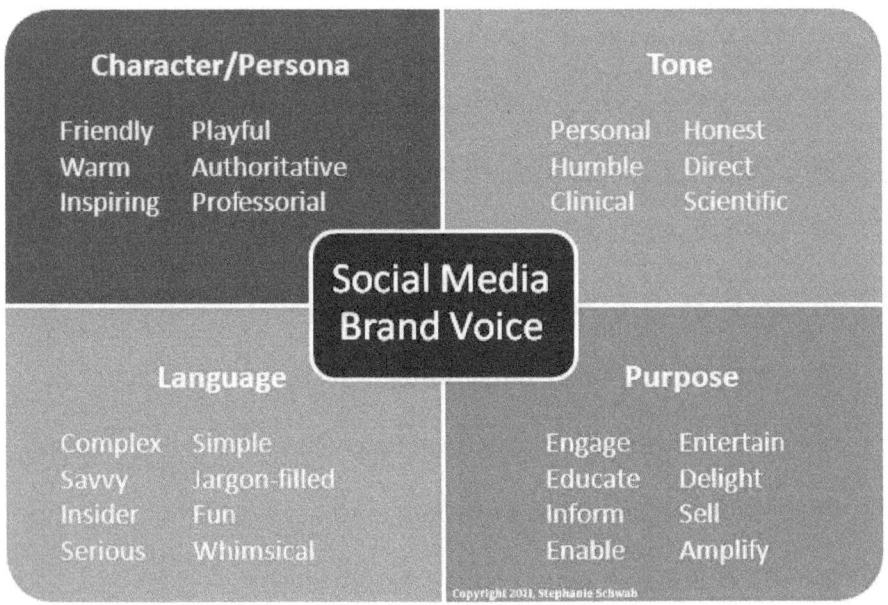

Character/Persona

Friendly   Playful
Warm   Authoritative
Inspiring   Professorial

Tone

Personal   Honest
Humble   Direct
Clinical   Scientific

Social Media
Brand Voice

Language

Complex   Simple
Savvy   Jargon-filled
Insider   Fun
Serious   Whimsical

Purpose

Engage   Entertain
Educate   Delight
Inform   Sell
Enable   Amplify

Copyright 2021, Stephanie Schwab

Looking to Fill Some Slots?

Best 50 Niche Job Boards

by SmartRecruiters on November 29, 2012 (reprint with credits)

Where to post job openings? Niche job boards attract top talent, giving you quality candidates with experience or interest in your specific industry. Niche sites to post jobs include not only niche job boards, but also niche communities and publications. In posting 350,000+ jobs for 60,000+ companies, SmartRecruiters found that 62% of open jobs are posted to niche job sites. Niches are just a good way to target whatever type of talent you are looking for.

Here are the **Best 50 Niche Boards** in alphabetical order:

 **37signals**

The 37signals job board focuses on programmers, designers, iphone developers, and business development jobs.

Post a Job to 37signals

 **AbsolutelyHealthCare**

Absolutely Health Care (also known as HealthJobsUSA.com) is one of the nation's premier niche healthcare and medical job boards.

Post a Job to AbsolutelyHealthCare

Adrants

Advertising jobs from your favorite advertising website, Adrants.

Post a Job to Adrants

**AllHealthcareJobs**

AllHealthcareJobs is a leading online career site dedicated to matching healthcare professionals with the best career opportunites.

Post a Job to AllHealthcareJobs

AllRetailJobs.com

The #1 Job Board for the Retail Industry

Post a Job to AllRetailJobs

Authentic Jobs

Where companies and creative professionals meet to make a better web.

Post a Job to Authentic Jobs

 **beautyJOBshop.com**

North America's online venue for Beauty, Spa, Salon & Fashion Jobs. Post a Job or Post a Resume today!

Post a Job to beautyJOBshop

 **Beyond.com**

Beyond.com is the one career network as focused as you are!

Post a Job to Beyond

 **ClearanceJobs**

ClearanceJobs is the premier secure job board focused exclusively on candidates with active or current U.S. government security clearances.

Post a Job to ClearanceJobs

CollegeRecruiter.com

Newest job posting ads from CollegeRecruiter.com, the leading job board for students searching for internships and recent grads looking for entry-level jobs.

Post a Job to CollegeRecruiter.com

 **coroflot**

Design-driven companies worldwide use Coroflot to recruit outstanding creative talent.

Post a Job to coroflot

 **Craigslist**

Local classifieds and forums – jobs, housing, stuff for sale, services, gigs, resumes, events, etc

Post a Job to Craigslist

CrunchBoard

CrunchBoard gives you access to the millions of technology and business savvy readers of TechCrunch, MobileCrunch, CrunchGear, TechCrunch IT and is one of the most popular job boards for internet and tech jobs.

Post a Job to CrunchBoard

**Dice.com**

Dice.com is all about celebrating tech and tech careers – advice, community and having some geeky fun.

Post a Job to Dice

DiversityJobs.com

DiversityJobs.com is a job search engine that finds job listings from company career pages, other job boards, newspapers and associations.

Post a Job to DiversityJobs

eFinancial Careers

eFinancialCareers is the leading global career site network for professionals working in the banking and finance industry.

Post a Job to eFinancial Careers

energyfolks

Energyfolks is a growing network of energy interested students and professionals from across the world's top universities.

Post a Job to energyfolks

FinancialJobBank

FinancialJobBank.com is the premier career site for job seekers and employers in the Accounting and Finance industry.

Post a Job to FinancialJobBank

FlexJobs

FlexJobs is an award-winning job site for part-time or full-time flexible jobs, such as telecommuting or flextime, in 50+ categories, entry-level to executive.

Post a Job to FlexJobs

Geebo

Nationwide free classifieds for housing, rentals, roommates, employment, jobs, vehicles, autos, sale.

Post a Job to Geebo

**GitHub Jobs**

Find the job you want. Reach the top programmers and developers here.

Post a Job to GitHub Jobs

 **HealthcareJobsite**

HealthcareJobsite.com is the premier career site for job seekers and employers in the Healthcare industry.

Post a Job to HealthcareJobsite

HireFlyer

HireFlyer.com is the top job search website solution online.

Post a Job to HireFlyer

iCrunchData

News, Updates & Jobs in Big Data, Technology, BI, Statistics, Cloud, Mobile, Software & Analytics. Unlimited Job Postings for Employers!

Post a Job to iCrunchData

InternMatch

Your source for the latest internship trends, tips, and access to great internship opportunities.

Post a Job to InternMatch

IT Job Pro

#1 IT Job Site, ITJobPro.com is a HUB for IT Professionalism world-wide looking for employment in Information Technology

Post a Job to IT Job Pro

JOBLUX

Joblux

Luxury Brands and Retail Careers Network.

Post a Job to Joblux

JobsInLogistics.com

The #1 Job Board for the Logistics Industry

Post a Job to JobsInLogistics

JOBSinManufacturing

JobsInManufacturing

For all positions in plant management, production planning, materials management, engineering, maintenance, purchasing and logistics

Post a Job to JobsInManufacturing

JobsInTrucks.com

The #1 Driver Job Board

Post a Job to JobsInTrucks

 **Juju**

Juju.com is a job search engine, not a job board. Juju's comprehensive search results link to thousands of employer career portals, recruiter websites, job boards, and other employment sites all over the Internet.

Post a Job to Juju

 **Krop**

Creative & Tech jobs.

Post a Job to Krop

 **Laimoon.com**

Bringing you ALL the UAE's career development opportunities! Follow us for the best jobs, education, and professional development advice & info

Post a Job to Laimoon

 **The Levo League**

Levo League is a thriving online and offline community of young professionals, role models, and innovative companies taking Gen Y by storm.

Post a Job to The Levo League

 **Mashable**

The Mashable job board is great for finding bloggers, consultants, designers, developers, executives, marketers, and mobile programmers.

Post a Job to Mashable

 **mediabistro.com**

Community, jobs, courses, news, and resources from mediabistro.com and beyond. Please note that featured jobs posted to this feed are #paid.

Post a Job to mediabistro

 **MyNextGig**

Express yourself with a 30-60 second video pitch and receive real-time job notifications and employment updates.

Post a Job to MyNextGig

 **paidContent**

Part of the GigaOM network, paidContent.org provides global coverage of the business of digital content.

Post a Job to paidContent

 **RecruiterMedia**

We offer a smarter alternative to the universal employment websites. We own RecruiterNetworks.com, the only national, city-specific, job board on the planet!

Post a Job to RecruiterMedia

 **Sales Gravy**

SalesGravy.com connects top sales professionals with organizations looking for sales talent.

Post a Job to Sales Gravy

 **SalesHeads**

SalesHeads.com is the premier career site for job seekers and employers in the Sales industry.

Post a Job to SalesHeads

 **Simply Hired**

We are a job search company whose goal is to make finding your next job a simple yet effective, enjoyable journey!

Post a Job to Simply Hired

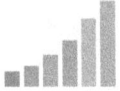

StackOverflowCareers

Careers 2.0 matches great programmers on Stack Overflow with great jobs.

Post a Job to StackOverflowCareers

**Taegan Goddard's Political Wire**

Post your political, government, and legislative jobs on the jobs section of Taegan Goddard's PoliticalWire.com

Post a Job to Political Wire

**Talent Zoo**

Since 2001, TalentZoo.com has been connecting top companies across North America with talent available in the advertising, marketing, and new media industries

Post a Job to Talent Zoo

TechCareers

Tech Careers

TechCareers.com is the premier career site for job seekers and employers in the IT and Engineering industries.

Post a Job to Tech Careers

Teens in Tech Labs

Teens in Tech Labs provides tools and resources to young entrepreneurs world-wide. Join the party!

Post a Job to Teens in Tech Labs

TipTopJob

TipTopJob is the Generic Job Board that covers over 35 industries – search and apply for jobs online

Post a Job to TipTopJob

VB

VentureBeat

The VentureBeat Job Board is great for finding people in IT, tech marketing and advertising, product management, and business development.

Post a Job to VentureBeat

YouTern

YouTern

YouTern connects emerging talent with dynamic start-ups, change oriented non-profits and passionate entrepreneurs – through internships!

Post a Job to YouTern

These are the **Best 50 Niche Sites to** Post Jobs. To attract talent that is driven to work in your industry and be the best in their field, post your job openings to the appropriate niche job boards, niche job sites and publications. With SmartRecruiters, you can post job openings to all these sites in one click. Post to niche boards today.

Ben Klafter, @BizDevBen, is on a a quest to partner with the best recruiting services. Got a great recruiting service or technology? Email Ben@SmartRecruiters.com.

Additional Helpful Links

Below are some links for further exploration and use in your professional campaigns and careers:

Create Space – Publishing resource

Hootsuite – Social media mass communication/tracking tool

TrustCloud – Social vetting tool with a bright future

So, you've read some credible information.

What are you going to do with it?

Do you have a plan?

Do you need help?

Can you bring yourself to ask for help if you do?

Where are you going to get the help?

We can help you... Be The Dream

Reach out to Zen on LinkedIn™: www.linkedin.com/in/zenbenefiel

 Zen Benefiel is an accomplished author, coach, facilitator and speaker who holds Masters Degrees from the University of Phoenix in Business Administration and Organizational Development.

Just after the turn of the century Zen helped women and minority-owned businesses garner over $200,000 in micro-loans through Self Employment Loan Fund. He assisted an indigenous coalition in Arizona to garner attention and inclusion in the development of the Steele Indian School Park. He managed logistics for large public events drawing over 250,000 patrons in his 30s.

Zen hosted over 100 television shows in the early 90s, called *One World*, inviting his guests to explore how we overcome fears and move toward harmony in our personal and professional environments. He also produced a four-host series of community activist shows, focusing on community activists, holistic medicine, youth empowerment, and straight talk on politics. Some of the shows are at: youtube.com/bethedreamllc

Mr. Benefiel meets challenge with style and grace as an opportunity to develop successful business and personal relationships, resulting in a highly qualified facilitator. His work as a *partnering facilitator* with Arizona DOT and Federal Highways Administration launched several high profile projects such as the renovation of Mather Point at the Grand Canyon, and for a Department of Defense contractor the F-35 Operations and Maintenance Facility at Luke Air Force Base.

He currently coaches, consults and facilitates client surveys, customer service, employee involvement, partnering, team building, strategic planning and professional development.

On the web, visit: www.BeTheDream.com (coach/consultant/facilitator), www.BeTheDream.info (blog), or www.ZenBenefiel.com. At the latter you'll find a host of other engagements and projects that continue to hold benefits for a growing number of people. Lastly, visit Zen's author page here: www.Amazon.com/author/zendor

www.ingramcontent.com/pod-product-compliance
Lightning Source LLC
Chambersburg PA
CBHW071756170526
45167CB00003B/1059